UNACCEPTABLE CHRISTIAN

Dez Demps

Unacceptable Christian

Details in some anecdotes and stories have been changed to protect the identities of the persons involved.

Cover design by Desmond "Dez" Demps and Daniel Zion

Edited by Elizabeth Maynard Charle

Copyright © 2025 Dez Demps

All rights reserved. No part of this book may be reproduced or transmitted in any form or by any means, electronic or mechanical, including photocopying and recording, or by any information storage and retrieval system, without permission in writing from the publisher. The only exception is brief quotations in printed reviews.

Hardback ISBN: 979-8-9992459-0-8
Paperback ISBN: 979-8-9992459-1-5
eBook ISBN: 979-8-9992459-2-2

This book is dedicated to my beautiful wife, Tymerial. My love, it was your words of encouragement that made this possible. I love you and thank God for you.

UNACCEPTABLE CHRISTIAN

CONTENTS

Foreword 9

Sand Dedication 13

Homeland Hate 19

100 Random vs 50 Consistent 25

To Sting or Not to Sting 29

Outta Reach 37

Face Value 45

Farewell 53

Actually Being There 57

Simple Marriage 65

Cinderella Man 71

Wrong Size 77

Shake 'N Bake 85

Relationships and Sex 91

Cartwheel Faith 95

Caught in the Bushes 101

Mountain Top 107

Bucket 113

Unfun Forgiveness 119

Dis-Located 123

The Best Part 127

Egairram 131

Oh Boy 135

Book Cover	139
Ready Ain't Waiting for You	143
Fear vs Ready	153
Just Another Tuesday	161
Unwanted Grace	167
Rags to Riches	177

UNACCEPTABLE CHRISTIAN

Foreword

You may be wondering why this book title is so provocative. Well there's a story to that. I have lived the life that seems like the perfect Christian would be proud of. I professed the faith at the early age of twelve. I started a Friday prayer in my high school. In college I led a Bible study called Young Vessels of God (YVOG) that was the biggest student led organization on campus at the University of North Florida (UNF). That was a sizable accomplishment, being a Black kid at a predominantly white institute).

I also was a virgin until I got married. I was even known for not cursing, with the key word being "was." I volunteered in the youth and young adult ministry and later become a youth and young adult pastor. At this point I've been in ministry for twenty-two years at the age of forty-two. I've lived the cookie cutter life that Christians are expected to live.

My issue is that I never felt like it was enough. Honestly, I never thought I was good enough. No matter how much I did, I just couldn't catch up to the expectations. I've counseled and helped people over the years but there was always a nagging depression that grew within. I felt imprisoned by the expectations. It wasn't necessarily by God but by man. I wasn't raised in the church, so certain moments of church etiquette were difficult for me. I always felt more comfortable with the world than I did in the church. I just knew I could never say that.

I felt comfortable with God, I just didn't feel comfortable with those who claimed to be his people. I had thoughts and ideas that were unholy, so I figured I must be unholy. I felt all the things they said someone of my dedication shouldn't feel. I wanted to curse. I struggled with pornography, and I was ready to fight anyone when I was aggravated. I felt like a walking double standard. No matter how much I tried, the acceptable mold of Christianity felt more and more like a prison.

At one point I lost my desire to do it all. It took me a long time to get comfortable with just being me. I felt obligated to be everyone's view of an example and not an actual person. Then I realized that if I was acceptable to God, it didn't matter who disagreed. I found myself on the other side of disappointing others' expectations. I found my true acceptance being unacceptable to those who had higher expectations for me then they did for themselves.

My hope is that you read this book and see yourself beyond the damaging culture of perfectionism that plagues modern-day Christianity. It's ok to be human. It's ok to have emotions. It's ok not to be fine when something devastating happens. It's also ok not to rush the process to quickly get to appearing like everything is ok. God gave us emotions for a reason. The day I realized feelings weren't a sin, is the day I finally began to live.

Take a short walk with me through this book. It's an honest conversation of what I've learned along the way. I will be addressing a variety of topics such as forgiveness, faith, marriage, etc. It's an honest moment to moment diary of lessons from an unacceptable Christian.

By the way, I hate feeling like I have to pull out a dictionary or a thesaurus just to read someone's book. The average listener does not have the same ears as a horn player who loves jazz because they don't play the music. Some authors write like this is their chance to show their intelligence and how many SAT words they can use. But it confuses us and makes the book instantly uninteresting. Well at least it does for me.

Trust me, I won't be doing that for this book. It's my first one, and the last thing I'm going to do is make it boring. Now I may throw a word in there every now and again to show off a little, but trust me, it won't be much. It's funny how God can use a person who has always had an anxiety issue with reading to write a book. I was the kid in class who got nervous when the teacher said, "Ok, everyone, we will have (insert your name) to read in front of the class." I'm getting anxious right now just thinking about it. I'm the guy that hates seeing subtitles in movies because I can almost never get to the end of one sentence before they move on to the next subtitle. I know it's nerves but for some reason I don't think I'm the only one. Things like that can make you feel less intelligent than others.

I write this book not from a place of insurmountable greatness, but from a seat right next to you. My hope is to unravel the hidden truths we subconsciously avoid and correct the hidden lies we often live by. In short, I am someone to be comfortable with. This is a journey for us both to go on and see what we discover. We'll use the buddy system. Take this like we are pen pals. For those too young to know what that is, shame on you for making me feel old. But I mean it. Use your pen as a bookmark as you go through the chapters. Underline and highlight phrases that stick with you. Write on the side of the paragraphs, above, and below the pages. Finish the entries, then go back and reread what you wrote and highlighted. It helps with memory. Let's have fun with this.

This book is written by a Christian man, but it is not penned in an orthodox way. I was raised to believe in Christ by a mother who taught me from a young age. She had to work, and often we took Sundays off to rest. In short, I'm not a church kid. We went when we could. My writing reflects that.

If you are looking for a book that is a little more cookie cutter, maybe this isn't the one for you. Some of these examples may make the normal church mother clutch her pearls. But if you stick with me and allow yourself to challenge the narrative you may have lived by, my hope is this book blesses you. By no means will I be living on the edge to mirror your average "shock jock." Instead, I have decided to be myself throughout this book.

Many Christians have a way they talk in front of other Christians and then a way they just talk when they don't feel like they are being judged. I'm breaking the fourth wall like Will Smith would often do in *The Fresh Prince of Bel-Air*. I'm just going to write the way I talk no matter what. I hope you enjoy.

My wife told me authors do this, so here are my social networks:
Instagram:@dezdemps
Facebook: Dez Demps
Tik Tok: @dezdempsofficial

CHAPTER ONE
Sand Dedication

When my wife and I got married, we didn't do the unity candle. For those unfamiliar with it, that's when a couple lights a single candle during the ceremony to signify them becoming one. I'm sure I'm oversimplifying it, but that's the gist of it.

We, on the other hand, poured two bottles of sand in the same holder. My sand was brown, her sand was tan. I liked it because it created beautiful lines in the clear holder. I tried not to shake it over the years because the more you shake it, the more you lose the lines that separate the colors. That annoyed me because I realized we didn't think it through. As time progressed it changed and became less and less like how it looked at the wedding. Over time moving it from place to place made it shake and mix the sand. A good portion is so meshed you can't tell the difference or even the dominant color. It started creating a new color that was a mix of both.

One of my favorite drinks from Starbucks is the Strawberry Acai Refresher with lemonade. It's best when you get it chilled because it tastes like a slushy. I noticed they put the strawberry syrup at the bottom. Because of that, the syrup swirls around the cup as you add the other ingredients. It looks sort of like how a candy cane looks when you leave it in the sun too long. I always tell them to mix it so it's consistent all the way through. That takes a little bit more stirring than they normally do, but it makes the drink more evenly distributed.

The Word of God says …

> "That's why a man leaves his father and mother and is joined to his wife. The two of them become one."
> (*New International Reader's Version*, Genesis 2:24)[1]

But the time it takes for the mix to be evenly distributed is what we seldom hear about. That's marriage over time. The shaking and stirring makes you more one. You don't want to shake the table but the shakes bring you closer together. You may not want the stirring to go longer, but whether you know it or not, it's making you more connected. It's ever-changing, ever-evolving, and ever-removing.

Food for Thought:
        We often describe what a connection will add to our lives, but we seldom address what it removes.

As the lines mesh, individual lines begin to fade. We are individuals but some of the negativity of our individuality gets removed. This unfortunately is where a lot of couples seem to fall because we have the assumption of only additions, when God has some subtractions on the agenda.

I won't talk about you, but I'll deal with me. I didn't know there were issues of trauma in my past that skewed my response to things. I thought many of my reactions to conflict were healthy. I had heard my whole life that I turned out well for all I had been through. I unknowingly internalized that as nothing has ever truly affected me. This created serious problems in my marriage. I was bringing a defense mechanism, camouflaged as a personality trait. A foreign enemy infiltrated the homeland of our oneness, and I was the one who invited it in. Removal is so important because it sets the stage for truth.

Food for Thought:

We say nobody is perfect as if it's the understandable excuse not to get better.

I got tired of apologizing for things I had no intent to change. Some behaviors are unacceptable. I learned in love sometimes the way to show love is to seek help for the issues you may have, so you don't hurt those you love. Removing the lines in a relationship is breaking down the barriers that hurt them, by hurting you, or rather hurting your ego. I know this sounds rough but it's true. I realized I couldn't see me on my own, but I could recognize my actions hurting my love. So I sought therapy first. In that I faced the hurt that was causing the pain in others.

One of the best things you can do to progress your relationship is to address the issues you don't want to face. Whether you want to see it or not, unresolved pasts tend to unravel unfinished futures. I'm spending so much time on this because maybe you are like me. You had so many expectations for your spouse that rarely addressed the expectations you should fulfill.

As the vase of your relationship shakes, the lines should disappear. But if it shakes and nothing changes, there will be issues. What part of you must disappear to maintain the new color that's trying to appear? Don't get me wrong ... you are not losing you. You are losing what was never intended to be a part of you. I believe a lot of relationships have failed over the years because the same statement is said with irresponsible expectations. We say "accept me for me." How can you expect to be the same but also mesh into one with another?

We all change. What if addressing your past helps you finally overcome your attitude problem? What if courageously seeing the pain shows you why you have commitment problems? Many personality traits are responses to experiences and not intentional decisions. Ask yourself where you would be as a couple if you finally dealt with what scares you to address.

No one is strong enough to not be affected by what is not addressed.

Love has many descriptive traits. One that is rarely spoken of is long-suffering. What if the long-suffering is you suffering for love—you bearing the burden of your past so you don't ruin your cohesive future?

Here's what that looks like: I love you more than the comfort of acting like it's not that serious. I love you enough to pay attention to the consequences of my unbridled actions. You are worth facing my inner demons. You are worth the tears that may fall. This relationship is worth the fight. I'd rather fight me then fight you. If removing the lines includes lines that protect my inner demons, I'm willing to let them go. Even if it costs me my comfort for a season.

Love gives you a reason to be a better person. You realize those lines were barriers that posed as boundaries. Letting go of the thing that kept people out will make room for your spouse to make it in. I was the type of person that said I'll give you most of me, but I will hold on to this part because no one is allowed here. But the two becoming one involves all parts of you and all of them. The more you get past the lines you tried to put up, the more you see each other's true colors.

When you are in a storm with someone, the first thing you do is hold on to them so you won't be separated in the chaos. If the wind is calm, you can stand next to them and nothing will happen. But in the real storm you hold on. Wherever the wind takes you, you go together. If you are tossed with the wind, at least you are together. The harder the wind blows, the tighter you hold on. That's how marriage develops.

Food for Thought:
    You can't control the storm but you can control how you hold on. The storm can take you into the air but as long as you have who God gave you, you are grounded. Any space in between can become a problem with holding on together through the storm. The only way to stay together is to omit the space between you.

Make sure you are not the cause of the space ... even if the truth hurts your ego. Hurting an ego has never caused any damage to anything other than pride.

CHAPTER TWO

Homeland Hate

In the silent era of the film industry there rose a star by the name of Charlie Chaplin. He became famous for his character "the Tramp." He was so famous that he was known worldwide. To this day he's regarded as one of the most important figures in film history. In the height of his fame he once entered a Charlie Chaplin look-alike competition. He wore his infamous outfit—a top hat, tattered clothes, and arrayed the same short mustache. With all of the same stuff on, you would think he would come in first place, right? Nope ... third. This was just as shocking to me as it is to you. How in the world does the original get mistaken for a third place copy of himself? How can a competition based on his likeness get it wrong?

Food for Thought:
People will have a moment of mistaken identity with you based on their inexperience with the real thing. They are convinced their opinion is so true that they present it like it's a fact.

Contrary to popular belief I don't think it's out of spite. People will mean well in their wrong assessment of you, yet still be inaccurate. Life will stand you up in a line and they will be asked to identify the great one in the room, and they'll pick someone else. People will inaccurately view your presence based on inexperience. It's just a confidently spoken wrong opinion.

A fool's most common trait is cockiness misconceived as confidence. So don't be fooled. I watched a reel that said an opinion is the lowest form of intelligence. These judges were probably Chaplin impersonators who "believed" they were qualified. They probably had years of experience in impersonating Chaplin. But impersonators can have years of imitation and still have no clue of the real thing. Those who think they are qualified to judge you are often wrong—wrong because there is a difference in the appearance of greatness and actual greatness. Just because God has the facts and blueprints to who you are, doesn't mean others won't have opinions. Never choose the opinion when the truth is available.

The prophet Samuel once came to a man named Jesse's house to anoint one of his sons as the next king. Jesse brought all of his sons out except the youngest. One by one each son was rejected by the prophet. Jesse was so convinced it wasn't his last child that he didn't even intend to call for him. But at Samuel's insistence, he summoned him from the fields. The youngest was so low on the totem pole that he was given the embarrassing responsibility of tending the sheep. It may not have been that Jesse didn't love him. He just couldn't see the greatness in him.

When that son finally arrived he was anointed king in front of all of them. I can only imagine the look on all of their faces, watching the oil run from the top of his head as Samuel poured it. That young man would later slay a giant by the name of Goliath. He would write multiple Psalms in the Bible, and would have a city named after him. You guessed it ... Jesse's boy was King David. He was regarded as "a man after God's own heart." When he was finished being anointed he was eventually sent back to the fields to do the same job as he did before.

Food for Thought:

    Even after proof, people who are too familiar with you

can stay stuck in their inaccurate opinion about you. Don't let that sway you. Some eyes will see everything else but you ... and that's ok because opinions have never stopped God's calling. Unless the called listens to them.

Here's a little something to ease the blow. Sometimes people need to be blind to you, because if they saw the truth, they might try to take advantage of you. It's necessary to blind those that would alter the course of your path in a negative way. Don't let the rejection sway you into a depression. Some rejection is just people volunteering to not be a distraction. Look at it as not having to remove them later.

One day in a New York subway a violinist played scores of beautiful music for forty-five minutes straight. He effortlessly played pieces extremely difficult for even the most tenured musician. Nevertheless, even with such apparent skill, he was passed by pedestrians as if he were invisible. One could even assume that there were those that might have been annoyed by his presence. A few people stopped for a moment to watch and listen, but most passed by and treated the music as they would elevator music. There were others that completely ignored him. In all the time he played, he managed to make $30.

Toward the end of his session a woman stood in front of him in awe. He continued to play for a few more minutes. At the end of the song, with bright eyes, she said, "I saw you play at the Library of Congress, it was fantastic." What she knew that the passing pedestrians didn't was that this was Joshua Bell. He is regarded as one of the greatest violinists in the world. Even the violin he was playing was worth 3.5 million dollars. Two days prior to this he sold out the Boston Theatre. Yet for some reason in this subway, playing for free, his greatness went unnoticed.

Food for Thought:
    You aren't the first time that people have mistakenly

ignored greatness. You won't be the last. You may be the right gift displayed in the wrong place. Go to the space that honors you. Never be afraid to leave the place that doesn't. Even if you've been there for a while. It doesn't matter whether its forty-five minutes, forty-five days, or forty-five years. Make the move.

I've heard this next example in a variety of ways but I'll try to make it my own, so bear with me. When I was a kid we used to go to the candy lady in the apartments. She would open her back door and there was a smorgasbord of candies, sodas, and even water. Now you know there was barely anyone looking for the water. If you wanted something to drink you got the little juices that looked like a barrel with the aluminum foil top. We all had different ways of opening it up to drink from it. I was notorious for making a little hole in the top and squeezing it to drink. But what really stuck with me was the price of the water. It was only fifty cents. (Shout out to Curtis Jackson III. G-G-G-G G-Unit! That was for any millennials reading this.)

I'm sure the water was priced too low because she knew it wasn't a highly sought after item. If we wanted water, we could get it from our apartments just a few steps away. She didn't even care that we could see the twenty-four pack bag in the back, proving how she was making a small profit off the sales. She knew it didn't matter.

My hometown is Jacksonville, Florida, and yes, I am a Jaguars fan. You laugh, and we will fight. Hopefully by the time you read this book, they will be a much better team than they are now. But that's beside the painful point. Despite being in steaming hot Florida, our stadium has no covering. There are many days we are literally cooking in those stands. On those days they are selling water like hotcakes. But the price is drastically different from the candy lady. There were bottles priced at twelve dollars. But the people still buy them. Even when you leave the stadium, there are always people on the sidewalk selling water as fans take the long journey to their cars. They often sell them out of coolers for two dollars. Many of the dudes who were selling water had the same exact water the candy lady had. It was just different in demand and desire.

The same product in a different environment will garner a different demand and respect. It's not that the item changed. It was still the same water, but somewhere else it was viewed differently. A poor man wouldn't give you a dime if you offered him water while he was swimming under a waterfall. But a rich man might offer you his Bentley for a bottle of water if he was at death's door in the middle of the desert.

> When Jesus traveled to his hometown to minister he was unable to do much because of familiarity. In Luke, he returned to Nazareth only to be rejected by those that watched him grow up. In response to their disbelief he said, "A prophet is not accepted in his hometown."
> (Luke 4:24b)[1]

It was amongst his own people that he was unable to do many miracles, because of their disbelief. In the same sense we must accept the hurtful truth. Some of the worst places to activate your true purpose are in familiar surroundings. It will be family and friends who are often too familiar with you to see who you are.

Even Jesus had issues in places that didn't believe in him. How well do you think you will do? Environments that don't believe in you will become a detriment to you recognizing the purpose within you. They will reinforce the devil's misinformation, which he desires to spread in your mind concerning you. You are not required to stay in places that refuse to honor you, no matter how long you've known them or who they are to you.

Belief is bigger than blood. Belief is bigger than old friends. Belief is the glue that holds a good connection together. Some strangers will see more in you than one who has known you your whole life.

As Jesus was speaking, some asked, "How can this be? Isn't this Joseph's son?" One thing people are notorious for is hating "change."

Someone will see a difference in you but refuse to change how they perceive you. They watched Jesus grow up in the neighborhood. They watched him as a teen. To them he was just Joseph's kid. But to his purpose, he was The Son of God. Jesus was dishonored to the point that in his claim they tried to throw him off a cliff.

Don't let familiar people kill what's in you. Your purpose will often offend mediocrity. People may even say how dare you come from where you are from and think you are more than this. They are right. You are more than where you are from if it is holding you back. You are more than people's opinions. You are valuable even in places that can't recognize your value. Sometimes it's not those around you that need to be removed. Sometimes it's you. Move on from places that don't have the ability to move on from what you used to be. Get a move on!

CHAPTER THREE
100 Random vs 50 Consistent

Imagine you had an ax and were trying to cut down a palm tree. If you had one hundred chops in random different places, more than likely the tree would be mangled but still standing. However, if you had fifty chops in one consistent spot, the tree would fall. This is the importance of consistency. It may be boring compared to being all over the place with the tree. But if the goal is to chop it down, then stick to doing the same thing that doesn't have immediate gratification. Eventually your consistent movements will benefit you more than randomly chopping at it to keep it interesting.

We will look at something and see it isn't finished after the first attempt and see a failure, so we try in another way. But what if it's working? This also explains why losing weight is so difficult. Progress without proper perspective will always be subject to inaccurate perceptions. The immediate gratification of seeing progress will not always be available.

Bruce Lee once said[1] "I'm not afraid of a person who knows 5,000 ways how to kick I'm afraid of a person who knows only one way to kick but he's practiced that one way 10,000 times." Mike Tyson once said that greatness comes from consistently doing what you don't want to do like you love it. The great Muhammed Ali was one asked about his workouts and how he trains. He said that when he does repetitions he doesn't start counting until it starts hurting. My question to you is where did you start your count?

I hate to admit this next part but it falls in line with this chapter. Believe it or not it took me ten years to finish pursuing my bachelor's degree. For those who don't know, it should only take four years to finish. I, on the other hand, had decided as a freshman that going to class wasn't as important as they say it is. Because of that, I lost my full ride scholarship and also had to change my major.

My associate's degree took me four years because I couldn't stay as focused in class as I would've liked. Later I came to find out that may have been due to a late diagnosis of ADHD. But that's beside the point. When I lost my way in college I had to drop out for three years to make money. I went back home for a summer and had to look so many in the face and admit I had dropped out. It was tough but I kept getting the feeling I needed to finish. Fast forward to the end, I graduated in the most unorthodox way. But I finished.

Why is this important? Too often I see people who have dissertations, books, and podcasts about becoming a highly successful person. They attempt to inspire you to be a more productive person but often end up discouraging those who are not like them.

Here's a truth that may be hard for a few to read, but freeing for others—being a success in one area doesn't make you a success in all areas. With that being said, one can also conclude that being a failure in one area doesn't guarantee you will be a failure in all areas. Our problem is that we all have a tendency to generalize a few of our experiences to all of our experiences. Failure in this job does not guarantee failure in another. Failure in this relationship doesn't guarantee failure in another.

I love to say that we will prophe-lie to ourselves about our next, based on our last. I'm not here for the "high achiever." Don't be dismayed by the self-help book that a socially awkward workaholic wrote. I know this is a lot of information, but it's necessary someone hears this. You quit on yourself because you don't fit the mold of the overachiever. You are a regular person with regular motivations. Like me, you've made embarrassing mistakes you hate to tell people. This has even become the reason you quit the thing you were meant to do. But let me be the example of what happens when you finish the hard thing.

I finally finished college and was hired by a nonprofit organization called Communities In Schools. I ended up having an amazing five-year career that was elevated not just by my college background but mainly by my people skills. I found that I was exceptional at team and program building. I would not have had that understanding unless I stayed inconsistently consistent with the same chop. I put the ax down multiple times. But when I came back to the tree, I chopped in the same place.

Don't get me wrong—I'm not saying don't try new things. But there are things in this world we are called to do that don't feel like we are meant for it. College and I seemed to go together like water and oil. I was a fish trying to swim in a pond with no water. I just had to learn to fight the feeling of inadequacy and keep swimming. I know that seems not to make sense but sometimes your purpose doesn't. You may ask, "God, how can I do this without the proper surroundings?" You may feel like this isn't going to work. That's why you quit in the first place. I remember fighting God for so long and trying to chop down the palm tree of success with other cuts. I found random things to take a chop at. But I couldn't get that stupid purpose off my mind. I knew I was meant to finish ... I just couldn't.

I told my wife the other day that fighting God's plan is like running on a hamster wheel. You can expel all the energy you want to divert the plan but you'll just end up in the same place you were before, only breathing hard.

Food for Thought:
    If God has called you to a difficult task that has yet to stop being difficult, stick with it. It's better to have three slow steps out of the hamster wheel than one hundred within it.

God's will is final, and many have wasted a lifetime running in place trying to oppose it. Take those hard three steps. Endure as the Lord develops your patience and long-suffering. Show God that just like he stuck by your side, you will do the same ... even if it's slow. Slow motion is still motion. God seems to love a good struggle story. How great is it for you to read a book written by someone who rarely finished reading a book because of undiagnosed ADHD, someone who struggled in college for years. We may be birds of the same feather. I told you my failures. Trust me ... there are more that I've either forgotten or simply just don't want to tell you about right now (shrug shoulders).

We often keep looking for more in ourselves as if the person we are isn't enough. You already have enough gas in you to drive wherever God is leading you. Gas is metaphoric for those who have the bubble guts right now. I'm a failure gone successful. I was uncomfortable in college until the very end. But how do you learn that you can do all things through Christ Jesus until one of those things is consistently doing the thing you never felt comfortable doing?

Food for Thought:
Destiny and comfort aren't always travel companions. Sometimes "uncomfortability" jumps in the passenger seat.

If you quit before, start again. If you quit again, start again. If you quit even after then, start again. Eventually one of those starts will be the beginning to the eventual end. My therapist once said, "Stop looking at it as starting over. You're just picking up where you left off."

CHAPTER FOUR
To Sting or Not to Sting

When I was a teen I would go over to a close friend of mine's house to play basketball. I nicknamed him Bobbo (Bob-Oh). He was more like a big brother. He was one grade ahead of me and a big burly type dude, but he had a heart of gold.

In his backyard was this small court that was no bigger than the size of your average porch. Needless to say he would win often because of the size difference. But I'll have to give it to him. He definitely showed me how to handle myself with a bigger opponent.

One day we were playing, and the ball went up in the air and hit a tree that hung just above the court. When I ran to get the ball, a sharp, sudden pain hit my ear. I'd never felt something so painful. I yelled out, and Bobbo came to check me out. He looked at my ear and saw that I had been stung. We rushed into the house to his mom. She grabbed some tweezers and removed the stinger but the damage had been done. Now what I haven't mentioned is that I am extremely allergic to insect bites and stings, so you can imagine the swelling. My ear was so swollen there were no grooves in my ear. All you could see was a hole. For reference there is a thing that boxers experience called a cauliflower ear. Mine was that times two.

I never knew whether it was a bee or a wasp, but I knew it hurt. I mistakenly hit the tree, disturbed its nest, and possibly suffered its last wrath. Why do I say that? I'm glad you asked. If it was a honey bee there are consequences to its wrath. Honeybees can only sting you once. Once the stinger is in your body, as they pull away, it's still connected to the abdomen and pulls the bee apart. It becomes the bee's last act. The thing it does in response to a disturbance is also the reason for its demise.

Once you hit the nest or show some type of threat, bees become relentless. If you ever find yourself running from a bee attack don't jump into water. Bees have been known to wait for people to surface. That is some kind of persistence. I wonder if they know beforehand that this sting will be the last thing they ever do. If they do not know, I wonder if they would continue their pursuit.

It's always funny to me how revenge can strand us on an island of a one-track mind. My own anger has gotten the best of me a time or two. I remember having a concert at a local club. The owner and I had known each other for years. We agreed on opening the club early so the band and I could set everything up. Surprisingly, on the cover day, we arrived and no one was there. We called him and his assistant, and there was no response. Now that was uncharacteristic of his people. Everything had always been up to par and professional. After about an hour we got a response. The issue was not him but someone on the team.

After about thirty more minutes a car pulled up. At this point I was admittedly fuming. Now as I've said before I'm a long fuse to an explosive device. I can let a lot go, but once I get to the end of the fuse, I'm ready to blow up the spot. Let's just say the fuse was close to exploding when the car drove up. A young man nonchalantly exited the car, and I spoke to him to see what happened. To my surprise he didn't respond. He walked right by me like I wasn't even there. As he tried to open the door with his key, I mentally clicked. The explosive went off and I went for what I knew in the moment to be the only option. In my mind I said, "If talking isn't your thing, I've got other options my guy." My rage can take me to places where logic has never held a residency. I know I'm not talking about anybody that's reading this so I'll just confess my sins if that's ok with you. Once I realized he was ignoring me, I began to walk over to him with every intention of resolving the issue without words. My father once told me that you know the coward before a fight because he's the one that talks the most. I don't know if that helped me or scared me, because I have a no talk policy. If I'm going to run up, I'm running up. What are we talking for? Hence the silent charge.

What I didn't expect was the power of a spouse. My soon-to-be wife saw the look in my eyes, and before I could take two steps, she grabbed my hand. Now prior to this encounter I didn't know that she possessed the Professor X power. But apparently all wives come with this power already installed at production. I've barely been held back by grown men from fighting. It usually takes about three dudes to keep me at bay. Even then, they have to prepare to hold for a long period of time. That's also why I prefer never to blow up because it takes a while for my anger to subside. But this pint-sized angel saw a forest fire in my heart and snuffed it out like someone blowing out a single candle on a birthday cupcake.

Her small hand was gentle but persistent with the G.I. Joe Kung Fu grip. No matter how I tried she wouldn't let me go. She knew I wanted her to let go but she refused as if to say, "I know you want me to let go but you are going to snatch your hand." She knew I wouldn't do that because I've always been careful not to hurt her because of our size difference. This little Xena Warrior Princess asserted a power I had never encountered before, and I was defenseless. I already knew she was the one but then I KNEW she was the one. I knew she could read me enough to see me on a destructive path before I could even step on the road.

Food for Thought:

As a spouse or friend it is your responsibility to be a protector of those you love even if it's from themselves. Of course this statement is within reason.

Had she not grabbed my hand I more than likely would've spent the night in jail for the second time. Don't judge me, that's a story for another time. Side note, jail food is the worst part of the stay. You'll have bubble guts for days. In others words, if you haven't been, don't go. I give it a one-star review. Anyway, if my wife had not grabbed my hand, I would've missed the success of a sold-out concert. That same concert was directly responsible for growing my name in the city. If the concert had not taken place, I would've wasted money that took me a whole year to gather. Furthermore, I would have had to reimburse folks for tickets that helped pay for the venue. There were so many things that would've been a fiery ball of dumpster trash rolling down the hill of my future like a growing snowball. I would've gotten my sting in, but at what cost?

> "My dear friends, don't try to get even. Leave room for God to show his anger. It is written, "I am the God who judges people. I will pay them back," says the Lord."
>
> (Romans 12:19)[1]

The Word of God speaks about us being angry and not sinning. At some point, wrath will become the temptation that seems worthy of your disobedience to God. Trust me, there are no ways to "get even" without the balance being uneven. You will suffer from what you choose to torment. You will be damaged by who you damage, even if they've already damaged you. Someone bothering you is not an invitation for you to attend to their demise. Turning the other cheek is necessary to allow God to fight your battles. Of course this is not a ploy to stay in detrimental situations. By all means walk away. Just don't let a grenade roll out of you hand back into house as you walk out the door.

For my ladies, hear me out. I often tell guys not to argue for long with a woman. Say what you have to say and move on. Don't get petty, because while you are arguing on a level ten she's barely scratched the surface of her level five. You have brought a knife to a gun fight. She's holding back words that can tear your soul out. What men can do with brute strength, women can do with words.

Food for Thought:
    It's interesting to point out that the very things God has given us as an advantage for our spouse, we, in turn, use as an advantage against our spouse.

For example, his strength should be her protection, while her words are his. Sadly it's often the opposite because wrath has given our bad side a permission slip to go to crazy town. The place meant for safety then becomes the worst war zone in our lives because of irresponsibility.

No one can help you like someone you love. Also, no one can hurt you like someone you love. Unfortunately, we spend so much time reflecting on being the victim, we seldom notice our part in the stings. While home is the last place we should seek to expel our wrath, it is often the first. I don't believe it's intentional, but we are often ignorantly irresponsible. I'm not saying "ignorantly" to be offensive. But I'm speaking to the root of not knowing. Ignorance is bliss when you don't have to notice the damage you cause. We don't notice how much we hurt people, because we are too focused on how much we hurt from people.

What's hard to hear is that's what probably happened in the people who hurt us. Sometimes to end the cycle you have to first notice the cycle within. In doing so you keep the pain you can cause away from your doorstep.

Food for Thought:
    Controlling our anger prevents us from being Satan's greatest tool in our loved one's demise.

* * *

"My brothers and sisters, you will face all kinds of trouble. When you do, think of it as pure joy. Your faith will be tested. You know that when this happens it will produce in you the strength to continue. And you must allow this strength to finish its work. Then you will be all you should be. You will have everything you need."

(James 1:2-4)[2]

In times of ridicule I like to remind myself that our savior was persecuted. We can't act like we didn't know these things would come. Persecution is a part of our journey, and if we respond to all infractions like we did in our old life, how are we then a reflection of Jesus? Remember he was lied on, beaten, whipped, and crucified by the very people he was sent here to save. We often sanitize the power of Christ to fit the box of our finite understanding. We see him in a way that is non-threatening and docile. At the same time that he was offered up as the perfect sacrifice for our sins, he still wielded the immense power of the cosmos. In a Thanos snap of a gauntlet he could eradicate us all into dust. Imagine the self-restraint it took to let the Crucifixion happen. We knew he had the power because he calmed the rage of a sea like it was nothing. He showed that having power isn't enough. You must know when to use it and when not to use it. Sometimes the greatest plight of the powerful is practicing restraint.

Food for Thought:

        If Jesus could endure the disrespect of those who owed him everything, you can endure the disrespect of those that may owe you a little.

My question is, is your revenge worth permanent losses? Do you have people around who will protect you from you? Or are you surrounded by those that throw gasoline on your forest fire? After you get finished stinging somebody, you always pull apart something in your own life. Revenge is like fighting a stronger clone of yourself. Whatever you hit them with will be returned stronger and harder. Remember this ... you can't reap a pain you've never sown.

CHAPTER FIVE
Outta Reach

My wife is what you would call vertically challenged or smaller statured if you will. We are alike in many ways but height isn't one of them. She's about 5 feet, 2.5 inches tall, and I'm 6 feet. Did you hear me say that with my chest? Side note, I have an opinion of my height.

Venture into my brain for a second. I'm the tallest of short people and the shortest of tall people. It's like I'm right in the middle.

One day I was in the kitchen talking noise to my wife. I said something slick to which she responded by saying, "That's it, so you wanna fight?" So this fun-sized, beautiful woman proceeded to put up her dukes with middle school kid-sized hands. In other words I was not even close to being intimidated in the slightest sense. But I was entertained to the point of a small smile rising on my face.

I just so happened to be grabbing one of my SuperBeets chews out of the bag, and the setup was perfect. I think she anticipated the coming threat. "Alright don't make me hit you with one of these chews." Don't worry, this was a usual day for us ... just two grown people that constantly act like teenagers with each other. If it really gets intense she knows I won't play fair and I'll clamp that leg in like a headlock and tickle her feet. Playing fair ain't my ministry in the war of wrestling.

She responded with big eyes and said, "Why won't you let me threaten you in peace?" I couldn't do anything but laugh. She pouted a little, then reached for a cup in the cabinet. To my surprise she said something I wasn't expecting, "Will you help me?" Naw I can't do it. How do you threaten me, put up your dukes up, then turn around and ask for help? The audacity of wives is beyond me at times. Just be bold with it. When I said no, she responded with, "Come on, don't be like that." Here's where the Jedi mind trick set in. As I refused to do said task, I found myself reaching for the cup that was too high for her.

I imagine she was in a long black cloak, wielding my resistance to her will while saying in a Palpatine voice, "Yes, yes that's it, succumb to the dark side of the force." If you understood this reference without having to look it up, know that we are friends now. High Five! With a smirk on her face she then said, "I could've gotten it if I kept reaching." Now of course she was joking but it hit me for some reason. Without my assistance, she would've never reached it. She's a grown woman so the growth spurts are over. She reached the full capacity of her height. Flat foot on the ground, she's not able to reach what she wants. Now for me it's an easy task. My genes afforded me what could be seen as an advantage in her eyes.

There is a toxic statement that travels around our society that I believe is detrimental to our beliefs. You hear it all over the place—you can do anything as long as you put your mind to it. But what if you weren't meant to do it. What do you do when you realize there are certain things you were not born to reach? How do you handle it? It has even led us to the horrendous misinterpretation of scripture.

"I can do all this by the power of Christ. He gives me strength."
(Philippians 4:13)[1]

Most Christians take this scripture like it gives us a license to do anything we want. Just sprinkle a little Jesus off your elbow on it and it'll be magnifique. But where's God's opinion on these things?

If we all have a purpose, then there are a multiplicity of purposes—which means we aren't all doing the same thing. This would mean that there are God ordained purposes that have nothing to do with you. We often talk about people making bad choices in sin. But there are those who make inaccurate choices in serving God as well. There are two desires within you: your flesh and your spirit. They both have their own opposing opinions. Here's a subtle but important secret. Your flesh doesn't stop having an opinion just because you got saved. Your spirit is saved, not your flesh. Its demise will still be the grave. That's why the Bible speaks of us having new bodies. But that's a conversation for people much deeper than I.

There is a narrative amongst young men that I feel the need to address. I've noticed a push for polygamy like none other these days. Men say no man can truly be satisfied by one woman. I hear it all. A man is not naturally made to want one woman. Now don't clutch your pearls when I say this next part, but essentially this is true. Also please, please, please don't throw the book. Fellas make sure you don't take this as a license to go take suggestions to your significant other. I will not be held responsible for how they respond, nor your sore face in the aftermath. So here we go. It is natural to want more than you are allotted for. We do have a natural desire for infidelity. Polygamy is a natural desire for men. But our faith is that of supernatural beliefs. That is the call. That is the point of the word supernatural. It's above the natural tendencies. It supersedes the natural primitive desires. It elevates us to a discipline that opposes destructive tendencies that will be a precursor to our demise.

Being a person who serves a supernatural God means you do not succumb to the nature of the flesh. Following God is to resist nature while simultaneously superseding it through Christ.

> "I know I've been a sinner ever since I was born. I've been a sinner ever since my mother became pregnant with me. I know that you wanted faithfulness even when I was in my mother's body. You taught me wisdom in that secret place. Sprinkle me with hyssop, then I will be clean. Wash me, then I will be whiter than snow."

(Psalm 51:5-7)[2]

We were born into sin. Those desires have what people like to call "needs" when they are simply strong unbridled desires. We will use a misinterpretation of the Bible to our advantage in a second, won't we? I've even heard the conversation that so many of the Bible's greats had multiple wives. But we skip over how much turmoil they had to endure because of that. I wonder why no one addresses how God only gave Adam one woman in the initial union of man and wife.

Some could say my wife could've reached the cup if she climbed the counter like many others have done. She's even done it before. But that introduces a danger factor. She technically can reach the cup but at what risk? We put ourselves in danger, reaching and attaining things we weren't meant to grab. If she falls, what was once a single task now becomes a possible emergency room affair. It's not always that you can't do something. Sometimes the question is, what are you doing to attain it, knowing you aren't built for it? I know friends in jail right now for trying a lifestyle they weren't built for, which is also why they got caught. We can achieve many things outside of God's will. You can even be successful in many people's eyes. But having stuff does not mean being blessed.

Food for Thought:

Owning things is not an indication of God's covering. Sometimes it's the devil's best distraction from your purpose.

What I have hated is watching people who claim to be used by God do the exact opposite. If you want to find the most holy people in the world, look to the church. If you want to find the most evil people in the world, look to the church. Some people are used by God to do his will. Others use God to do their will.

They are so hungry for power and fame that their depravity reaches the point of using God to get what they want. They sing gospel songs to get well known. They preach to gain fame. They go into the Christian world of entertainment to get all the things they tried to acquire in the secular way. This is why you can't trust every gospel song. You can't trust every sermon. You can't read every book. You have to ask God for discernment to know how the things you ingest were created. What spirit were they created in? There are those that say Lord, Lord every day and do not know him.

In Genesis God commanded the people to fill the Earth. Instead, they decided to come together, build a city, and build a tower that reached the heavens. If you read closely in chapter eleven they were doing all this for fame and pride. Scripture even says "how good and how pleasant it is for brethren to dwell together in unity (Psalm 133:1 KJV)[3]." But here the unity was used in disobedience to God's command. They were commanded to do one thing in his will but unified in a way that can be seen as great but totally unholy.

Food for Thought:
  Be careful reaching for good things that aren't God's things.

When Eve ate of the fruit in Genesis 3 she first saw that it was "good" to eat. We can assume it was because after her bite she offered it to her husband.

No one offers terrible food to someone they love. But a good taste doesn't mean it's good for you. Anti-freeze kills a lot of stray dogs each year. The issue is that it is surprisingly sweet to taste. So when it spills from a car onto the street, dogs drink it. What if your desire/downfall is as sweet as you imagined it to be? What if the sin matches what you imagined it would be? How do you then refuse it after the first taste is heavenly? You have to remember it's still just as deadly.

Adding sugar to poison won't stop it from killing you. Be careful what you reach for. It could be a fun experience but a fatal one to your dreams. Not to be morbid, but I imagine our disobedience is like a man's last meal on death row. It's often exactly what they want, but it's just before the end. Before you start something outside of the will of God, ask a question: What will end? Is this your dream's last meal? Disobedience uses a cover called pride to hide a bad decision.

Take it from our ancestors who decided to build that tower. In their efforts God came down and confused the languages of man. It was later known as the Tower of Babel. Babel in its original context sounds like the word "confusion." By definition it means "a confused noise made by a number of voices." Confusion has a sneaky way of hovering around disobedience.

One phrase that destroys people is, "It's not that serious." It's not that serious, I can go to church next time. It's not that serious, I'm only a little late for work. It's not that serious, we just went on a date. But God said no. He never said they wouldn't be friendly. He never even said you two wouldn't have chemistry. I'm about to go off the deep end for a second, but bear with me.

Food for Thought:
Be careful. You can have sexual chemistry with people who are not the one.

These bodies are a randomized combination of old genes that have been passed down for generations. This creates variables of variables where two people who are otherwise not meant for one another can find a connection physically that feels right. But feeling right and being right are two totally different things.

It is true you can have chemistry in a flesh sense with a destructive person. It is your soul that is truly unique, not your flesh. That's how you can look like people in your family. Your flesh is not unique. Somewhere along the line you received every physical gene you have from someone in your family. But this doesn't mean you aren't unique. It just proves your identity doesn't start with your flesh.

I always marvel at the fact that Adam and Eve didn't even notice the nudity of their bodies until after eating the fruit. I assume they were so intertwined by their souls that the flesh was on the back burner. Making decisions for God is key to us not going down side roads that are hard to come back from.

Remember, sin is disgusting to God, not us. That's why we often fall to it. Some decisions in sin are harder to pull away from. Sexual sin has a multitude of believers in a chokehold because we slept with the wrong "right" person. We do our best to wait until marriage because we don't want to find poison that's too sweet to stop drinking.

Transparency moment warning: it ain't deep and barely Christian, but it is my truth so this may be my confession time.

I'm currently on a weight loss journey, and it's been up and down for years. I'm now 293, and in my last checkup I was told I had lost four pounds. You have no idea how much those four pounds mean to me.

One of the reasons I couldn't lose weight before is because the lies I told myself weren't working. I told myself that I wanted to lose weight because of health … didn't work. I told myself I wanted to be an example for those around me and post before and after pics … didn't work.

Then one day I sat and really thought about it. I don't care about any of that. I want to lose weight so I can stunt again. For those that don't know, that's a Black person's way of saying, "I want to enter a room and leave them breathless."

A former member of the Spice Girls, Victoria Beckham, had an interview that changed my goal. She's married to the famous soccer player, David Beckham. She said that once she saw her husband get out of the bed naked and walk to the bathroom. In her head she told herself, "Good job." I want that for my wife. I want to randomly get out of the bed naked and for her to say to herself, "Girl you did that." I know this isn't what you expected but it's my honest truth.

The acceptable answers we tell ourselves to not feel bad are making goals difficult. If you are on my journey you don't want to admit you really want to make heads turn again. You want to make a change because that trivial thing in others' eyes really matters to you. You might as well admit it to yourself. Be honest, you're already thinking it.

Maybe the honesty will help you with your true level of self-awareness. Sometimes we are so deep that we are of no earthly good. Being real with yourself is freeing and humbling. Maybe we won't judge people so hard if we admit how we really are. Sometimes we are constantly reaching for things we shouldn't, because we aren't self-aware of what drives us. Ask yourself, "Why do I want this?" Being real with yourself might help you make better decisions.

CHAPTER SIX
Face Value

When I was younger I did a lot of things for the Lord. Please pardon me, but this next part is going to feel like a slight brag although I promise it's going somewhere. I led a Bible study on the campus of the University of North Florida. At this predominantly white institute, the Bible study was the biggest club on campus. We had a small group for men and women. We had a dance and step group. I led an executive board comprised of roughly ten to fifteen students. We even went on road trips to conferences and concerts. We hosted huge parties and even had an awards banquet at the end of the year. I did counseling after Bible study and took calls from people often to pray and give guidance to those who needed it. In a nutshell, I spent a lot of time in my anointing.

Most days I was helping someone by seeking God for advice to give words of encouragement. It reminds me of when Moses went up on the mountain to meet with God. This was when the Lord gave him the Ten Commandments. When he came down from the mountain he had to cover his face because it was too bright for the people. His time on the mount in the presence of the Lord had left a residue of God's glory on him that needed time to subside. I spent a lot of time on the mount. I spent a lot of time in my gift. So when I came down the glory was still on me. But in that flaws can hide. I did so much work for the Lord my deep issues were able to hide.

The Word says gifts come without repentance. Even sinners can function within their gifts. So of course I can function in my pride and still be gifted. Funny how many character flaws can hide in the man of God when he refuses to come down from the mount. I was forced to ask myself, "Who are you beyond your gift?"

Food for Thought:
    Some of the most anointed people can be the most hurtful and judgmental.

I know because I was one of them. I wasn't going to outright judge you in words, but internally I had a haughty spirit. I judged you drinking too much. I judged you smoking. I hid it by saying God isn't with that. I was helping people so much that I didn't see that I needed help. I spent so much time in my gift that I didn't know me. I ran from my personal trauma by helping others with trauma. I avoided personal growth by avoiding personal healing.

I had issues and still do, but I remember a time when helping others was really my way of escaping the pains of my past. My mom once asked me to come home for a reason that I can't remember for the life of me. I told her I wouldn't be able to because I had gospel choir rehearsal. This was around the third or fourth time I told her I was too busy because of ministry.

Then she said something to me that has rocked my world to this day. She said, "Don't hide behind God."

Now the "college me" was offended. I was shocked to the utmost. How dare she say that. You can always hide behind God. Younger me was too prideful to get it. That's not what she meant. She was saying don't use God to be your excuse not to do what you are supposed to do. If you are reading this, Momma, I finally got it.

You see, my excuse was I'm committed to Bible study, choir practice, and any other ministry I could get my hands on. But the truth was I didn't want to come home out of resentment toward my parents.

My Pastor, Bishop Terry Hill, once said, "There is no such thing as 'My Truth.' There is just truth, and that's it."

You can create what you want to be true all you want to, but the truth is still the truth. Don't use God to avoid the truth. You can't avoid paying your rent because you said you had to pay your tithe and an offering. Naw, that's fiscally irresponsible. You can't think being in church five days a week instead of home will make your marriage better. Go home. If it's the first ministry, why is it getting the least time? Handle that bad attitude before you claim to be a messenger for God.

The "that's just how I am" excuse is causing damages in the kingdom that don't affect you but affects those you try to help. If you have a haughty spirit (note to self) deal with that before you judge people. In other words, sweep your front porch before you come trying to clean my house.

> "You look at the bit of sawdust in your friend's eye. But you pay no attention to the piece of wood in your own eye."
>
> (Matthew 7:3)[1]

Self-reflection is so important to faith but so undermined. Some of the most anointed and gifted people have the worst attitudes because of it. You may think, "Well Dez, I hear you but it's hard to see me." I get that, it was hard to see me, too. I'm still trying to see me better.

Self-awareness is difficult because no one wants to be the villain in their own story. How can I accept that I've projected my issues on to others as a means of self-preservation? It's painful sometimes to admit that at the end of the day sometimes there is no one to blame but yourself. That's hard for anyone.

What do you do when you seek to avoid the truth that you actually are a bit much? Where do you go when you are forced to admit they may be right about you? A young lady I counseled was bothered because people said she had an attitude problem. She said people were taking her personality wrong. She was confused because she felt like it was her against the world. I told her something that left her quiet for a while. If multiple people who don't know each other are saying the same thing about you, then nine times out of ten there is viable truth to it. In short, the crowd isn't always against you.

Instead, sometimes they are telling you the truth that you'd rather be offended with than take accountability for. I get it. It's easier to just be offended than hear the truth. It's easier to be a victim than to admit to having an issue. I hate to say it but some of the best relationships have been lost because a real friend said the truth and the other friend chose offense over admittance.

I'll ask you this as I've had to ask myself. How much have you lost being overly sensitive to mask your rebellion against accountability? It's the easier road but it's inevitably a lonely road because it eventually pushes everyone away.

Sometimes your self-reflection needs assistance. Long story short, I went to therapy. It changed everything. I needed help and found out that it's ok to need help. Pride will camouflage your actions so you can't see the pain you cause. But the humility will lead you to assistance that will open your eyes to your truth.

Now I know I said there is no such thing as my truth earlier, but let me clear that up. Some will say this is "my truth" to express what they view things as and what they desire for it to be. But your truth is simply what it is whether you want it to be that or not. It's the real you without blinders to the negatives. That's a difficult truth to face if you've always found comfort in the world you created to protect your ego.

To be clear, we don't always protect our ego out of being haughty. Sometimes it's to avoid pain. That's why needing help is not a bad thing. Therapy is so taboo for people, but I believe it is essential for personal growth. I know this seems like a strong statement but I'll ask you this. After all you've been through, do you really think none of it affected you? You changed after it and have never been the same since.

Maybe a barrier was created that you called "being stronger," yet you are really just being calloused.

The Bible speaks of a calloused heart. Callouses are made when a piece of skin endures a trauma and the skin responds by becoming harder to protect itself from future trauma. How hard have you become since someone rubbed you the wrong way? In truth this proves that harder doesn't always mean stronger. Do you know the difference within yourself? Do you really believe all of that trauma amounted to nothing, or are you avoiding revisiting what happened? I'm not here to stir up past pains. I'm trying to free a good heart that may be misrepresented by a calloused outer shell.

Unhealed pasts are open wounds. Open wounds tend to fester within the soul. You may have learned how to avoid it but it has grown on your personality like a parasite, without you knowing. We hear people say, "Why don't you trust anyone?" The easy response is "I just don't." But the truth is that the last time you trusted someone it was so devastating you vowed to never let anyone in that close ever again.

Food for Thought
     Be careful. Some of us make vows in response to pain that causes more pain in our lives.

Reopening yourself is scary but it is necessary. American actress and film producer, Viola Davis, once spoke about going to therapy to better herself and not necessarily for any particular traumatic reason. That motivated me to do the same. Sometimes Christians can over-spiritualize our lives so we don't have to address hard truths. We can create a world of toxic positivity where we don't accept our personality issues and say things like, "I'll just leave that to God." No, sometimes he's left that to you. Our character flaws are our responsibility.

American actor and rapper, Will Smith[2], once said that "It don't matter whose fault it is that something is broken if it's your responsibility to fix it." Our trauma may not have been our fault but the character damage of the trauma is our responsibility to correct. But no one said it has to be unassisted. My wife once said that "it's interesting how we will go to the doctor if we are sick. We go if we break our leg or need surgery. We go with all the parts of the body. But we just pray about the brain."

Food for Thought:
     Your brain and head space need more than prayer, just like those other things do. We will say, "God I need help with this," and he's saying, "Help is available now. Go sit on a therapist's couch."

I know this is therapy heavy but too many of us need it and downplay our struggle. Look at it this way: What could one session hurt? At the least you can prove me wrong, and the therapist will say there is nothing going on. I'm ok with that. However, more likely than not, in the realms of trust, success, and relationships, your past has affected you more than you think. It molded your drive, personality, and characteristics. You think you are batting 1,000 with everything you've been through. You think with all you've endured, none of it jaded your outward expressions toward others.

Instead, maybe you'll finally be able to unravel and be free of that thing you've been locking away in the back of your mind. You know the thing. The thing you can't seem to get over or let go. The thing that everyone keeps telling you to move on from but you can't. I've been there.

I didn't know my past changed me. I was living as though my facade was my personality. I didn't even know the difference between it and the real me. Many of us have created the facade to protect us and it's been protecting us for so long we don't know who we were before it was created.

Hear my heart. You are worthy of who you are without having to push down what you've been through. There is freedom. You just have to go get it.

CHAPTER SEVEN
Farewell

My wife and I pass by a Piccadilly next to our apartment on a daily basis. Honestly the lot is usually so vacant that we thought it was closed. But one day my wife was passing by and the parking lot was packed. Come to find out the restaurant was closing, and everyone was trying to get their last Piccadilly meal. My wife told me if they would be at the restaurant this much on a regular basis they would not go out of business. But there are so many people that pay no attention until you suddenly say they will have no more access. Now all of a sudden they want to give you all the attention they weren't giving before.

In relation to a business, the management could be tempted to open back up and forget what led them to close. Be assured as soon as they decided to open back up, those people who ignored them before would do it again, and the loss would be greater than before. In comparison, as individuals we want to be open to the right people and not the ones that have multiple instances of proven irresponsibility with our hearts. Some relationships come to an end for a reason.

Food for Thought:
        Don't get amnesia when a person's toxicity decides to show you attention when you close down access to what you can serve.

As soon as you do and they get that one meal, they will go back to ignoring you until you threaten closing again. No love survives on that cycle. If your lack of access is the only thing that attracts them, they are not worth your time.

In Atlanta there was a store that was going to close, and social media was going crazy because all of these new people decided to go and revive the company. People from all over the city went to buy products and it was beautiful. It actually saved the owner's business. I watched in awe of the community coming together. This was amazing. But what about tomorrow?

Of course the hype was about the moment. It was beautiful for the day, but what about the next day? Businesses must have a consistent flow of customers to stay open. Be careful.

As with businesses, people will see you closing and latch on to the excitement of keeping you open to them. They will show up out of nowhere as you are putting those memories in boxes, ready to take everything. For a moment they will gas up your dreams and look like they are in it for the whole journey. But as soon as that tank of gas gets low, you will look in the passenger seat and see no one there ... just like it was last time. They gassed you up to leave you hanging. Now you have to take the long journey again to walk back to your sanity, serenity, and peace. The key is to make sure that when you are closing one chapter, never let them reopen the book.

Lock the door while they are knocking on the window and drive off with the little gas you already have. You are better off with what you have than what they can offer.

People seek the toxic thrill of regaining access to people they have no intention of sustaining. They hear your bitterness when they call. They will endure your yelling and venting. They will give you the ear you have been waiting for them to offer. They will be who you wish they were the last time, just to prove these words in their head, "I still got you." It's a game narcissists love to play that has nothing to do with love and everything to do with control. Some people do not care about the damage they cause as long as they are permitted to play the game.

A phrase comes to mind—it takes two to tango. The game can only be played if another participates. You have to realize that the game appears one way and actually is another.

Food for Thought:
People who love vicious cycles don't return with power. They return to regain power.

As your doors close, the power shifts. You now have the upper hand to your life. There is a rotation to the narcissist. They return for a moment to moment stay for a few weeks or months, then inevitably disappear. Do you think they then live a life of solitude? Of course not.

They are thrill seekers so they are off to their next victim for their third time in the cycle to do the same thing. It's a Ferris wheel at Coney Island and they expect to get on whenever they feel. But what happens when you close the gate? What happens when you say no more? What happens when you say I am no longer a short fun ride? I am a long journey. I need you to expect the attention. Expect the calls and texts. Expect the knock on the door. There is nothing that gets the attention of a person that shouldn't be in your life like "access denied."

You may be thinking, "But I hear that inner voice creeping up. This sounds great, preacher, but I get lonely sometimes. I get tired of sleeping in a cold bed. Keeping it a buck, I also have an itch that though they are trash as a person, they are amazing at scratching."

No worries. I got you. Let's all be honest. Just because you know better doesn't mean you do better all the time.

For these instances I've created what I like to call the barrier system. It's the part that allows me to feel human, but gives me easily accessed truths that make it hard for me to fall again. I'm not always successful, but I'm a lot more successful with them.

For instance, write down what made you leave before. Write down how you felt the last time they came into your life and ruined it. Write down how embarrassed you felt. Write down all the confirmations you had that they were not to be in your life.

Now write down why they should come back. Nine times out of ten that first list will outweigh the positive. We don't fall back into something because we are stupid. We fall back because distance makes the heart grow fonder. We tend to forget the pain and fantasize the impact of a few good memories.

It's interesting how loneliness has the ability to overexaggerate the positives in a toxic person. Don't let the crowd of compliments and gestures sway you. Business is closed. If they say, "I miss you," respond by saying, "I missed me, too, and I'm not losing me again for you."

They can knock on the windows. They can slide money under the doors. If it was confirmed then, it's confirmed now. You don't need closure with them. You can do that on your own. Sometimes closure brings people who need distance a little too close. You can forgive someone without them being in the room. But you may not be able to conquer your desire while they are there.

Moving on comes at the cost of your present desire. It comes at the cost of satisfying your temporary needs to fulfill your necessary needs. Unhealthy relationships can be fun in the moment but will be painful in the inevitable end. Move on before the reminder of why you left in the first place is a reinjured heart.

CHAPTER EIGHT
Actually Being There

I wrote this the day after President Donald Trump won the election in 2024. No worries depending on who reads this as I won't be getting in too deep with politics. But I know that in light of Vice President Harris's loss, there was a lot of emotion and pain in the eyes of people. The airways and social media platforms were littered with two extremes.

One side was ecstatic, while the other was devastated. But I must admit, there was one thing that annoyed me through it all. It was the "God is still in control" people. Now hold on before you throw the book in the corner again in fear of lightning strikes. Let me explain.

My wife and I went through a hard season in our lives that changed us forever. We became pregnant in 2019 and it was the life of the party in our house. I laughed at her cravings. She was getting the beginnings of that pregnancy glow. We told a few people but kept it hush for the most part. One day we were sitting in our living room, and she began to bleed. She rushed into the bathroom, and I watched my wife have a miscarriage over the toilet. This would be the first of three over the course of the next four years. It was a hard time for both of us. It was also in the time of the COVID-19 epidemic. We were newlyweds facing a monster that usually eats most marriages alive.

By God's grace, prayer, and counseling we are still together today. However, a piece of us was changed forever because of this. If you know my wife you know she loves children, and the one thing she wanted more than anything was to be a mother. Unfortunately, after meeting with a specialist, we discovered it was highly unlikely in the natural means.

We sought out in vitro fertilization (IVF) consultations only to find that the expenses and invasive procedure seemed too much. We weighed our options and considered enduring the possibility of all that effort only to reinjure our hearts with disappointment.

Some dark places are hard to speak of, let alone revisit. I dare not be this detailed for a venting session. I'm just trying to paint a picture for your understanding. As months passed we metaphorically licked our wounds only to be bombarded by another unexpected issue— people.

We were making strides in accepting the possibility of not having children. But for some reason, that wasn't the desire for those around us. We had been married at this point for about five years and of course the next question was, "When are you two having kids?" This is not a terrible question but you would be surprised to hear how aggressive people can be when they are too invested in your life.

We were constantly reminded of a pain we were trying to get over. But we were also made aware of how women are viewed. The expectation of motherhood is unfortunately like a rite of passage. There is a very real undertone of "you are not a woman unless you have children." It got so overwhelming that I put a warning shot on Facebook that basically said leave my wife alone on this subject or else. It's still up, too. I meant what I said. Now let me kickstand for just a second. I am cool and calm in many ways. However, I don't play about my wife. The old me is dead but resurrections do happen when you come for my baby. Kickstand raised. Now let's continue with God.

When you see organizations support a random plight, there is a reason. There are organizations that head up things like research on breast cancer, domestic violence awareness, or to save our youth. The majority of those organizations are led by people who have suffered something parallel to the purpose of the organization. They help in research because they knew someone who suffered without it. They lead in programs helping with street violence because they lost someone in that manner. There are a multitude of great programs in this world simply out of the pain of a founder's tragedy. It made them sensitive and passionate toward the subject.

More than likely those founders would not have created these institutes had they not experienced what it was like to endure the pain of the lack of assistance. Pain often causes a specific empathetic sensitivity. It can allow for an understanding that wasn't present prior to the experience.

No one searches for people who don't understand what they're going through when they are going through it. The camaraderie of understanding helps in hard times. It almost allows the comforter to know what to say and do around those who need comforting. There are also those who desire to comfort without knowing how to. I don't know what it is but for some reason people need to be needed when they aren't needed. People will know they have never experienced something but still feel like they can discuss the subject. It's ok to admit you wouldn't know how to address a person's suffering. But there is a slithery issue that has infected the faith. It's pride wrapped in encouragement.

Christians will say, "I don't know what you are going through but God is able." I'm not questioning intentions, here, but even bad decisions with good intentions are still unacceptable. If I am showing you my new shiny gun while pointing it at you, I'm still responsible if it goes off. My intentions won't stop you from bleeding out. I'm just here to get brothers and sisters to unload the gun and point it at the ground.

I'll never forget the audacity of a woman at our old church. She knew me for a short time but had never spoken to my wife. There was an after-service event where she walked up to us and began asking about us starting a family. We said our usual response, "We'll leave it in God's hands," but she wouldn't leave it alone.

She kept saying, "I've prayed for people and they've become pregnant." She swore up and down that she had the touch. She then, without asking, reached over and touched my wife's stomach, speaking over it as if to express her power.

I'm glad she removed it quickly before I could grab her. I calmly walked her to the side and told her to please refrain from the subject. I wasn't mean or aggressive, but I made it clear we would rather not discuss that especially at this time. Interestingly enough, she apologized but still insisted she had a gift. Side note—God is not a genie that we can just summon his power whenever we desire. But that's a conversation for another day.

A few weeks had passed, and there was another event in our church's gym. She approached me, wanting to discuss it again. My wife was out of earshot. I calmly reminded her of the subject's sensitivity and asked that she not approach my wife with this topic. She claimed to understand, still adamant about her praying power, but agreed to leave my wife alone. A few moments later, I saw her talking to my wife in the distance.

Now, I told you already that I have a glitch in my system for my wife. So I headed straight for the table to say everything but what the Lord desired to be said. I had warned her. Now she was going to see the unhinged part of me that God delivered me from.

Walking closer, my wife noticed me in the distance and waved me off. I wasn't hearing that so I kept walking. But she looked again, and I knew what was happening by the look on the lady's face.

You see, I'm the brutally honest guy. I'm the "blow up the spot and not care about the damage when I'm angry" guy. However, that little fire cracker of mine is a calculated assassin. The lady hadn't anticipated that my wife had been waiting on her to try it. She gave her grace the first time because I was a leader in the church. But the second offense after warning deserved a specific response. All I could do was watch her dismantle this overzealous woman from afar. I couldn't wait to hear about it later.

At the end of the conversation, they hugged it out but you could see the sweat dripping from the lady's forehead. There is a thing that married people do when they are far away from each other but can see each other. We can speak with our eyes and facial features without saying a thing. So I looked at her from afar and said, "We good?" to which she responded back with, "Oh we good."

Lady, I tried to save you. Apparently super sister walked over there, pretending it was to apologize, only to further push her claim to a power that could get us pregnant. However, she wasn't expecting a simple line my wife hit her with. What if our pregnancy is not God's will? What if this is my burden to bear. What if this is for his glory?

She had nothing. She had never considered that. Left speechless, she was schooled in the understanding of how we must submit to the will of God whether it's our will or not—that just because she was weary, her disposition did not mean her faith was failing. She was just being human.

Food for Thought:
> Surface level faith expects God to do what makes sense to us. Real faith is accepting what doesn't make sense to us as long as it's his will.

> There we go—I know you were waiting for this long story to make a little sense eventually. She was throwing all kinds of scripture and common clichés that most believers know, at us. I disagree with this approach wholeheartedly. Too often we rush to the ministry of encouragement before we address why the person needs encouragement. I have a theory: truly being there for people is uncomfortable for the person being the comforter. Consider this scripture.
> "Be joyful with those who are joyful. Be sad with those who are sad."
> (Romans 12:15)[1]

We want to enjoy every experience with someone as they rejoice. We want an invite to the party. We want to be in the thing they are celebrating. It's fun. It's entertaining. It makes us feel good.

But when they mourn, we want to throw scripture at them from afar like throwing rocks at a pond. We hope the ripples do something but we are not getting in. God has called us to sit with our brother and shed tears with them. In other words understand what it feels like. Feel why this time sucks. It's in your empathy that you realize how to truly be a friend.

In the book of Job when Job's friends came to comfort him in his time of trouble, they just sat with him in silence for days before saying anything. What's funny to me is that we act like the person doesn't know the scriptures you want to say. They often know them. They are just having a tough time because it feels like they aren't working.

Psalms 34:19 says, "The righteous person may have many troubles, but the Lord delivers him from them all.[2]" It's a tremendous scripture but it highlights that the righteous will not go through life unscathed by trouble. It comes with the gig. There is overwhelmingly more joy than pain but pain, nonetheless.

Nobody responds to pain with a smile. It's ok to respond to trials. It is also ok to allow people to respond to their affliction without a rush to scripture. You'd be surprised at how effective a listening ear, a sit in silence, or a simple hug can be.

The garbage man comes by our house once a week. I had to get used to taking the trash to the curb on Thursdays. If I would forget, then we would have to keep a few bags in the house because the bin was too full. I couldn't put more in it. I would have to wait until the garbage man came to empty it.

Don't be so quick to pour into someone if you haven't already allowed for them to be emptied out. Let them get the pain out before you pour in. In their vent, you also get a clear understanding of what God may want to put into them.

Contrary to popular belief, you are not so anointed that you can know everything they need without listening. Only God can do that. We are not little gods. We are God's children. When God knew we needed his help to reconnect us to his glory, he came down in human form to die for our sins. He wrapped himself in the disgust of our flesh and endured all we could handle. Then he bore a burden we could not handle. He mourned with us in our situation, then saved us.

Supernatural Christian, you are a testimony of God's grace. But never forget your human form. Be there for those who are suffering. Understand their suffering. When Jesus was on his way to the cross, he was so beaten, dehydrated, and weakened, he fell carrying the cross. An African man was called to help him carry it to Golgotha (the place where he was crucified). The man helped Christ carry the burden. He didn't stand to the side looking at Christ yelling, "You can do all things through Christ who strengthens you."

I know that last sentence is a little weird because he is Christ. But you get the gist of what I'm saying. Love is far more than your personal comfort. Being there takes effort. Don't take the lazy route.

CHAPTER NINE
Simple Marriage

I may get in trouble for this one … but if you get offended, please keep reading. It gets better.

Ladies, if you want a good marriage, just make sure your husband is happy. That's all that matters. If he's happy, you will be, too. It doesn't really matter how YOU feel. Just make sure he's good. Offended? Why? Reverse it. Now you see the toxicity of "happy wife, happy life." The better saying is "Happy Spouse, Happy House." It matters because you both matter.

Food for Thought:
So many of us seek marriage as a gift but rarely seek to be the gift in a marriage. To be a gift is to make sure the present on the inside matches the beauty of the wrapping on the outside. Excuse my dialect in this next sentence, but I am from the South. Is it about you or is it about y'all?

I'm going to dive into something a little different for clarity. You can't be someone's therapy if you haven't first had it yourself. You can't fully expel peace unless you have it yourself. I bring this up because I believe it's a necessity for becoming the best you that you can be.

We often stop at church and sit down with the pastor, however, if you break your leg, your first call isn't the pastor. It's the hospital. We have a sickness, so we call the primary doctor. We have a disease, so we get medicine, but if we have trauma in the mind we pray about it. Some of the weight we carry, we've been carrying for years, so we don't even notice it. But what you don't notice in you, everybody else does. Trauma is always a blinder to self-awareness. You won't even be able to see how you are toward those you love.

There are those that say things like, "Yeah I've been through a lot but look, I turned out ok." Let me be honest with you. A good job, going to church, a good spouse, beautiful children, and the white picket fence with a dog are not the indicators that you are OK. It could be evidence that you survived.

I'm a huge action movie buff, and it's not a good movie unless the hero gets hurt a little. The best ones are when they survive bullet wounds and almost being blown up. But for those, they usually end the movie in some scenario where their loved ones are surrounding their hospital bed as they recover from their injuries.

I think many of us have some action-packed history. We've been through a lot, and because we are still here, we think it's over. But unlike the movies, we don't allow for the recovery part at the end. We skip over that and prepare for the sequel.

In the movie industry it's often said that most sequels are not as good as the first movie. In the movie *Den of Thieves*, Ice Cube's son, O'Shea Jackson Jr, plays a criminal mastermind opposite Gerard Butler's character who tries to stop him. However, Butler's character suffers a lot in the first movie. *Den of Thieves 2* has been announced, and Butler is slated to now join Jackson in his criminal activity. Here's the interesting twist. Without recovery, the hero becomes shades of the villain in the sequel.

Compare this to your own life. The pain is too unbearable to be the good guy you were in the first movie. I'll ask you this question: Have you fully healed from your first heartbreak? Or are you shades of the villain in your sequel.

This is why recovery is so important. Even God put an emphasis on the importance of recovery when he rested on the seventh day. Now we know our all-powerful God doesn't need the rest. But he knew the importance of showing us its impact.

Without recovery you will become the villain in your own story and won't even know it. The best villains rarely, if ever, know they are villains. For those who have watched the *Avengers: Infinity War & Endgame*, you know that the powerful titan, Thanos, thought he was doing right by eradicating half of the population in the universe to help it thrive.

Don't close the book when I say this next sentence. Putting your heart aside, you can analytically see where he's coming from. There was overpopulation on many planets, so removing half allowed the others to flourish. The question, though, is at what cost? The eradication of some to make room for others is barbaric. A time of peace after barbaric feats to achieve said peace will always have negative residue in the peace attained.

Those barriers created to protect you were viewed as necessities to maintain your peace in hard times. It benefited you in protecting you from those you deemed would harm you. They protected your peace. Or did they? It appeared right because the walls kept the bad people on the outside. This is true. But what you didn't realize is that it keeps the good people out, too.

Like Thanos, it was an extreme answer to harness peace, but it came with an extreme cost. You have to ask yourself, how many people have I lost at the expense of extreme measures to garnish peace? Here's a harsh reality. Walls don't provide peace. They provide isolation dressed in solitude's clothing that will inevitably lead to loneliness. Walls come with distant and defensive attitudes.

Imagine if you were running full speed but didn't notice an invisible brick wall in front of you. The injuries would be terrible. More than likely, you would also choose not to go that way again. The risk of pain would not make it worth it. That's what happens when people are running to love us. The walls of rigid words and actions create injuries.

They walk away because it hurts too much to keep trying. We will wonder, "Why are they walking away? I didn't do anything." You are right. You didn't. But your wall did. It's not you, but because it surrounds you, it's your responsibility. You could have intentions to be a way to those you love and still miss the mark.

Sadly many of us choose to be offended before we are accountable. For example, if I'm playing with a gun, and it goes off and shoots you in the chest, an apology won't stop the bleeding. I saw another example on Instagram that reflects this. If I throw a plate on the ground and it shatters, I can say I'm sorry to it 1,000 times. It will still be shattered on the ground.

We often use apologies for glue when personal change allows for the glue not to be needed in the first place. True apologies are when the offense is noticed and a change in behavior follows.

Food for Thought:
Apologizing with no effort to change is simply reciting the right answer to keep the peace until you do it again.

Now before this gets too judgmental, let me be real with you. I was one who would apologize with little to no intent to change. It was the right thing to say to just move on. Funny enough I went through a season where I was so low for other outside reasons that I sought therapy. What I thought was meant to help with anxiety and depression, helped with so much more.

The sessions showed me things I didn't realize were hurting me. My therapist revealed thought processes I had that I thought were universal, but they were just personal. I walked away from our sessions a renewed man. I was better for the world and namely better for my wife. I could clearly see some of the things she had been trying to tell me for years. I was even able to see things I needed to change and the damage I caused from my own personal drama.

I was the one who constantly said, "I'm fine." But I didn't know I wasn't until I met with a specialist for the mind. I learned how to think about what I was thinking. I know it sounds crazy but learning the roots of your thought processes helps with deciphering between good thoughts and bad thoughts. Sometimes we think we know the difference when we really don't.

What if some of the ways you think about your relationship is based on incorrect teaching? I was offered the opportunity to see myself outside of some ways I thought were correct. Weights were lifted that I didn't know were there. I know this chapter took an unexpected turn. It was titled for marriage but it turned into a push for personal growth. In truth that's what makes it even more relevant to marriage. The best way to improve your marriage is to improve yourself. The best way to correct a marriage is to correct … I think you got it.

CHAPTER TEN
Cinderella Man

One of my all-time favorite movies is *Cinderella Man*. It's about a boxer named Jimmy Braddock who is played by Russell Crowe (the guy from the movie *The Gladiator*). The time period is the early 1930s during the Great Depression. Jimmy was a highly decorated fighter which earned him and his family a nice home and prominence. But as times got harder they had to move to a smaller rundown apartment in Jersey City, New Jersey.

He worked at the shipyards between fights, lifting bails with a hook. Struggling to pay the bills and feed his family, he eventually was able to get a fight. He was known for his vicious right hook, but his left was terrible. He looked good in the fight as it progressed, and that's when tragedy struck. While swinging with everything he had, his opponent dropped his head. Hitting the top of the boxer's head, Jimmy broke his prominent right hand. Remarkably, he continued to fight with the broken hand.

Understandably, he was less aggressive and more protective of his hand. This lack of action created a stir on the crowd that ended in boos and thrown popcorn on the mat. Immediately after the fight they revoked his boxing license due to the fight being such a disaster. This left him devastated. All he had left was the shipyards. The only issue was that his prominent hand was in a cast. Every day men were fighting for shifts, and with a cast it would be even harder.

He used shoe polish and painted the cast black and carefully hid it under his sleeve. Before the fight he would use his dominant hand to hook the bails. But because of the injury, he was forced to use his left hand. He continued this until the right healed.

After a while, his former trainer showed up to his home with an opportunity. The current contender for the title was in need of an opponent because the guy he was set to fight had to drop out. The gimmick the trainer proposed was for the contender to knockout a guy (Jimmy) who had never been knocked out.

Truthfully he sold that just so Jimmy could get a fight. The bell rang, and the two began throwing gloves. Jimmy was obviously rusty. He had no time to train, and he was older. The contender was in peak shape. But what seemed to be an obvious win, turned out to be quite the opposite. Gloves were swinging all over the place between them. Then the contender swung a vicious hook that knocked the sweat from Jimmy's brow, and his mouthpiece flew out of his mouth to the floor of the ring.

It's clear the boxer had hit him with everything he had. Jimmy's vision became blurry, and while it cleared, he began to have flashbacks of his past few years. He had visions of the hard times. He saw his decrepit home. He saw his three children. He saw his wife at the sink washing dishes. He saw his "why." While all of this happened, the contender bounced around smiling because he knew he had bested his older opponent. But that smile fell when he noticed another smile in the ring across from him. Jimmy started smiling like a crazy man and managed to pick up his mouthpiece. It was as if to say, "That's all you got?"

The fight continued but it was a totally different fight. Jimmy began destroying the contender and finished him with a left that even shocked his trainer on the outside of the ring. After the fight, the trainer asked, "Where did that left come from?" To which Jimmy responded with a grin, "I must've picked it up from the shipyards."

He found a new skill in his worst times. He found his left. My question is, what's your left? What are you gaining in your hard times? You might even be in a job you don't want in this season, but it will give you skills necessary for your next. This is not your end and don't despise your small beginning. It's tough now but what's now, won't be always. At rock bottom Jimmy gained things that caused him to do more than what he could have done before.

When seeds are planted they must be buried in dirt and darkness. It is there that their full potential is able to flourish. The nutrients of the dirt and rainy days are the perfect place to develop what was in them the whole time. The sunnier environment just wasn't quite right.

I can imagine that seeds would rather be above ground in the sunlight to see the beautiful day. But they will never reach their full potential without being buried and enduring some necessary rainy days. What if I told you that you are not being pummeled, you are being planted. You are not being demoted, you are molting.

Caterpillars are confined to the darkness of a cocoon for a season to emerge as the beautiful butterfly. The interesting thing is that although the caterpillar looks nothing like a butterfly, that butterfly DNA is still in it. It just needed the right environment for those genes to manifest. What if this hard season isn't a punishment? Instead, it may be a cocoon. It's not rock bottom, it's just you being planted. You've been buried away from the sunlight but eventually you will see it again. Then you will be rooted and sturdy.

Flashbacks of your struggle will give your fight purpose. Maybe you'll be like Jimmy and lose your right but begin to develop your left. When you feel like things don't feel right you'll find out what you have "left." I think we should read that last sentence one more time.

I heard one of my favorite sermon examples at an assembly at William M. Raines High School. Jon Heymann, the former CEO of Communities In Schools of Jacksonville, had a basketball and held it up for us all to see. He said, "If I removed all the air from this ball and dropped it, it would stay on the ground. But if I fill it with air it will bounce." He then dropped the ball, and it bounced back in his hands.

He then said, "But if it is filled with air, it bounces back. It needs a certain amount of pressure to bounce from the ground." It's the pressure that helps it to bounce.

Food for Thought:
    It's when things get tough and you feel the pressure that you gain the potential to bounce back.

He said the ball had to hit the bottom to bounce. That's the thing about the bottom. The only other place to go from there is up. So if you are at the bottom, you know the next direction. The pressure isn't there to take you out. Neither the pressure nor the bottom are where you will end. It's there to help you bounce back.

Embrace the storm. Jesus was once asleep at the bottom of a boat as a storm was on the water. The storm tossed the boat back and forth but somehow he still managed to stay asleep. I bet you didn't know that your savior was a heavy sleeper. All jokes aside I think he stayed asleep for a reason. He was only awakened by frantic calls of scared disciples who were afraid it would sink.

Often I hear people dive in to Jesus calming the sea after this ordeal. But we often skip over the fact that the storm wasn't a concern for him. I wonder what would've happened if they had never awoken Jesus. Would they have sunk? Would they have drowned? I'm inclined to disagree with that notion because his purpose wasn't fulfilled yet. His purpose was to die on the cross for our sins, not die at sea. Your purpose is to die to your flesh, not die in this season. We have to realize that if God's not concerned, then neither should we be. If he's relaxed, then you can relax.

Food for Thought:
    Sometimes God is quiet. We wonder why he's not talking in light of the hard times. Sometimes this isn't the time for talking, rather it's the time for trusting.

Excuse the vernacular but if God ain't done, then you ain't done. Trusting the process doesn't mean that the process is going to always feel trustworthy, but still trust it. This is not the day you lose. It's the day you lose your fear and fight. Everybody loves to recite Isaiah 54:17[1] "No weapon formed against you shall prosper."

Yeah the fight is fixed. But what they don't tell you is that you will get punched. You will get punched more than once. You will get hit in ways that make you want to drop to your knees. You may even get hit so hard that your mouthpiece falls out. However, the guarantee is that if you endure until the end, the score cards will unanimously announce you as the winner.

It's good news at the end of the fight but terrible in the middle of it. Watching the rounds go from one to three is easy. But what if God decides he wants your fight to go the distance? We all want the Mike Tyson fight—the fight that lasts for no more than a round. What do you do when you expected the fight to be over at round six but now the woman walks around the ring holding up a poster that says round ten? What do you do when the rounds are still going?

I loved a cartoon in my youth known as "Pinky and the Brain." At the end of every single episode Pinky would ask Brain one question: "What are we going to do tonight?" This to which Brain would respond, "The same thing we do every night, Pinky. Try to take over the world!" No matter how hard they failed the previous night, it was always Brain's hope and determination for success the next night.

Well I'm not Pinky, and you are not Brain, so we are not here for the entertainment of kids. You will not suffer the same fate as they did but you must maintain the same fervor. They never achieved their assumed purpose but you will. When that unexpected round comes walking around the ring, think with hope, "the same thing we do every night" knowing one day you will. Don't go down because you always have something left.

One of my favorite rappers, Lil Wayne, said, "What's a goon to a goblin." I'll ask you this: What's a storm to a purpose? What's a temporary problem to a permanent solution? Your purpose always outlasts troubles, and storms are always temporary. Sometimes purpose uses darkness for development.

When I was in high school one of my favorite classes was photography. We were given cameras and were taught how to develop the film in a dark room. Why they thought it was ok to allow high school students to go in a dark room by themselves, without supervision, is beyond me but that's a young Dez story for another day. The Lord has brought me a mighty long way. Back to ministry ... I almost lost my Jesus for a second in a flashback. Anyway, what is real is that the film could only be developed in the dark. The sunlight would ruin it. Then after it shows smaller on the film you are able to look over the film, approve the images you want, then transfer them to paper for bigger images. When we dipped the sheet, it stayed white, then eventually the picture began to show. Sometimes it's not until after you allow yourself to develop that you are able to get the big picture. You may not see it in your dark room, but trust me. Something in you is developing. This isn't your end. It's your beginning.

> "I know the plans I have for you," announces the Lord. "I want you to enjoy success. I do not plan to harm you. I will give you hope for the years to come. Then you will call out to me. You will come and pray to me. And I will listen to you. When you look for me with all your heart, you will find me."
>
> (Jeremiah 29:11-13)[2]

CHAPTER ELEVEN
Wrong Size

This past Saturday I was buying some groceries and passed one of those automatic blood pressure machines. Out of curiosity, I parked my cart, sat down, and stuck my hand through the arm slot. It was a little tight but I managed. I pressed the button and heard the buzz as the machine began to slowly cut off my circulation for no reason. At least that's what it felt like.

It pressed so hard I just knew something was wrong with the machine. Then it stopped and gradually backed off my arm with small syncopations. I could feel my heart beat in my arm and waited for the results. All of a sudden it released, and the results came on the screen — 163/120. Wait, what? I paused for a second, then tried it again. Same result. After the third try, I did what everybody else would do. I looked on Google to see if I was reading that correctly. Everything I read said, "Medical emergency, seek immediate medical attention."

I then called my wife to see if I should be concerned just to be sure. After pausing from initial shock, she told me to use the machine we have at the house. For clarity, we have one for her in light of previous blood pressure issues. But I, on the other hand, had never had issues. She was sure the machine was off. Nevertheless, I rushed home. (Don't worry about the rush part. Some speeding may have been involved, but don't let the devil use you to judge me.)

Anyway when I arrived home she came downstairs and wrapped

my arm with the same strap she uses. It took a second for some reason. We kept having to reapply the strap, but it eventually worked and we were able to start the machine. It showed the same numbers. The air in the room immediately left. We both got quiet and tried it again ... same numbers. She looked at me with concern, and I looked at her, trying to appear like I wasn't concerned. But truthfully let me help you see where my mind was.

In the past two months I had buried my fraternity brother (my Dean for those familiar with greekdom) after he had heart problems. A few weeks later my father went to the hospital with a heart attack. Needless to say, my mind had a lot of references for freaking out. Now back to the drama at hand. After three of our own failed tries at home, we reluctantly decided to go to the emergency room. When we walked in, they put the plastic identification bracelet around my wrist and told us to wait. Everything else was fine until it wasn't.

A lady was rushed in screaming at the top of her lungs, "I NEED HELP!" They sat her in a wheelchair and she began yelling multiple one liners for the next hour at the same volume. What was interesting was she was accompanied by an older man around her age, and he was as cool as a cucumber. The medical staff moved as fast as they could but she was still saying things. Her verbal playlist ranged from, "YALL ARE TRYING TO KILL ME" to "OH IT HURTS" to the old classic, "I SHOULD'VE GONE TO A DIFFERENT HOSPITAL." From the lack of rush in the medical staff and her husband, I could tell some other things might have been at play. She was definitely trying to bull rush her way into assistance.

The wait would've been easier if she had let me stay focused. She also showed her hand when she (a white woman) yelled out, "MAYBE I'D GET SEEN IF I WAS A DIFFERENT COLOR." I leaned over to my wife who was looking at her phone and said, "Did she just say what I think she...," to which she responded before I could finish, "Yup." At this point the jig was up. We knew something wasn't right. You may ask why I added this to the story. To be honest I just wanted to. It annoyed us and I wanted you to be in on the annoyance. Yup that's right. Misery loves company, and thank you for listening to my TED talk. Admit it, you had fun though. Now let's get back to the main event.

We were eventually called back to a room, and the wait continued until they came in to take blood. I hated this part because ... wait, nobody likes this part. We all hate the thought of being poked by a needle. The nurse began to check my arm for veins and seemed to have trouble. She then found one, so here came the needle. It was a slight pinch but I could feel the needle moving further and further up. It wasn't working. Of course I knew what was going to happen next. She had to try again. Poke ... push ... hope. Thank God this time it worked, but when I looked down, I saw a small mess of blood. At this point I was questioning the nurse's skill. But I was just glad it was over.

Later, the blood work and EKG were done, and about an hour later the doctor came in. She said that I had what is called a first degree heart block. No worries. It sounds worse than it is but at the time it sounded like I was done. It is said to be the least severe heart issue, and often people live their whole life not knowing they have them. But the high blood pressure was still a concern so they suggested I see my primary doctor immediately. She also suggested I needed to prepare to take blood pressure medicine.

When we made it home, we scheduled the appointment for Thursday. So, from Sunday to Thursday all kinds of things ran through my head. I mentioned my fraternity brother who passed. Well what I didn't tell you was that I was the last person to see him alive. I visited him in the hospital on a Saturday night. He was scheduled for a surgery for blockages in his heart on that Tuesday. He passed Sunday morning. So relating to that real experience, I feared the worst. What happens if I don't make it to Thursday? They were telling me about symptoms I was expected to have. I wasn't having them prior to this, but with each day I felt more symptoms manifesting in my body. I felt more fatigued. I was getting headaches. My heart felt like it was about to bounce out of my chest a few times each day. I questioned everything. Externally, I looked cool and calm, but internally I feared leaving family and friends. However, I feared leaving my wife more than anyone. The thoughts and feelings I had were awful.

Thursday morning finally made its appearance after a few days of horror. They took me to the back, and of course the first thing they did was check my blood pressure. The nurse took out a large band, wrapped my arm until I heard the Velcro, and then did something different. She took out a stethoscope and placed it on the inside of my arm. All I could think was oh that's old school. She placed the earpiece into her ear and began to listen. She then took the earpiece out and astonished my wife and me with the next thing she said ... 130/80. Say what now? We were dumbfounded. Of course I was thinking how in the world can that be? But a faint yet relevant memory came creeping up from the back of my mind. I'd been to the doctor before with a nurse who was a burly man who seemed to be of Samoan descent. He took my blood pressure then, and said something I had forgotten about. He said that I needed to be mindful to ask those taking this test on me to get the bigger bands because of my size. For context, I'm six feet tall and weigh 295 pounds but I have a very solid frame. He said that normal bands will often have misreads on guys like me. Now everything made sense. I'm not the average sized person but I was measuring myself on average sized instruments and getting incorrect readings.

Food for Thought:
There are many of us who are misreading our whole lives based on the average size of faith that everyone else has.

You measured yourself on the average actions of the people that surround you and have been getting inaccurate readings for years. My wife and I were sitting there with our mouths to the floor. I told the nurse what was told to me before, and she confirmed that it was correct. When my primary physician, Dr. Wright, walked in, he did his own blood pressure check, and the findings were the same as the nurse's. He then told us everything was fine and sent me off with an order for an XL wrap.

In school we learned that a noun is defined as a person, place, or thing. How much drama are you inviting into your life simply because you are wrapping your arm with nouns that don't fit? What malfunctioning noun is at your side causing you to misread your current situation? Had I been checked by the correct wrap, I would've saved myself a lot of time and discomfort.

You will always find nouns that have no problem telling you their measurements of you. The problem is whether the measurements are right. You have to ask yourself what is wrapped around your arm and is it giving you the right readings? Birds of a feather may flock together but do they fly? If you are trying to fly, make sure you are in the right flock, in the right place, doing the right thing. If an eagle walks with a flock of ostriches, it will have trouble keeping up. Their legs are too long, and if they decided to run, it becomes more difficult. Even worse if the eagle is able to keep pace, it then will become dangerous. The ostrich could step on the eagle by accident. It's not the ostrich's fault. It's only doing what it was meant to do. It's the eagle that is keeping the company that can hurt it.

If you are meant to fly, you can't measure yourself by things that are meant to walk. They will be dangerous to you and will make you feel "less than" because you can't keep up with their level, on their level.

I remember back in my twenties, a friend and I were hired at the same time for a nonprofit organization. We both excelled at the job but for some reason, he was just better. We both were promoted to management positions amongst twenty others. I was able to reach a well-respected level of success, but even then, he just stood out among all of the managers. He received multiple awards and accolades for his work. I worked my behind off, but honestly I couldn't even be mad at him. We had become so close that we called each other brothers. He even joins my fantasy football league every year.

Eventually, I ended up leaving the company for full-time ministry. I stayed in ministry for the next decade as he continued on his journey in the company. Eventually he took the position of our former boss. As he rose, so did I in my dream in ministry. We both had the same drive for excellence. He just found his place in his position earlier than I did. But there was no room for jealousy or comparison because it wasn't my purpose.

I think many of us miss the mark because WE become the malfunctioning equipment. We start to measure who we are by the people we are next to, and jealousy gives us misreadings when that's not even what we want. I've seen ladies get mad at their friend for getting married first. They get jealous of seeing their happiness and seeing them have loving moments. The funny part is that they are often jealous of them having a spouse they wouldn't even want, so why be jealous of somebody else's success?

Now I know a few of you may be saying that ain't necessarily true because I know of some people who are jealous of someone else's spouse because they do want their spouse. Well that's a story for another book. I never wanted to permanently be where my brother was meant to be. He was excelling in his purpose, and there was no need to side-eye him for his success. There was also no need to measure myself by his success. That's why when it was time for me to leave, I was able to function well in my purpose just like he did.

Food for Thought:
    The only thing that should measure who you are is the God we serve. If he is saying well done, then that's all you need.

I said before, that when I was waiting for my doctor's appointment and tests on that Thursday, I was starting to have symptoms. It doesn't make sense after getting the clean bill of health. I look back and think of the days I was afraid to walk or do anything because I was afraid to raise my blood pressure. I seemed to experience almost every symptom they told me about

As soon as we got the news that my readings were normal, I immediately felt fine. It was like a weight left my body. Instantly I didn't feel my blood pressure. I didn't feel dizzy. I didn't even feel a hint of symptoms directly after I was told everything was ok. I was suffering from the stress and worry of a phantom sickness my mind had convinced my body that I had. I was so convinced, that symptoms I had not previously had began to manifest.

In many controlled experiments involving people there is a studied pill and a pill called the placebo. The studied pill is the one that contains the substance to be researched, and the placebo has no substance. Neither group are told which is which. What researchers have found often is that the placebo group will still have measurable differences based on the fact that they were told there would be a change. Imagine how powerful that is.

Food for Thought:
The power of suggestion is so strong that there is quantifiable evidence that changes happen based on belief.

Now apply this to your life. How many symptoms are you experiencing based on suggestions and not facts? How many assumptions are you believing like they were facts? What part of your life is in shambles because the wrong noun presented false evidence of a lie it wanted you to believe? It said you would never be anything and you accepted the placebo like it was the real substance.

Your faith says that you are fearfully and wonderfully made (Psalm 139:14)[1]. By the way, faith itself is the <u>substance</u> of things hoped for (Hebrews 11:1)[2]. So when you hear something that lacks substance, stick with what God tells you. Nothing has the authority to shrink what God has for you.

CHAPTER TWELVE
Shake 'n Bake

When I was a kid, Shake 'n Bake was a popular seasoning that came in a box. All you had to do was buy meat. You would then open the bag with the seasoning, place the meat in the bag, seal it back up, and shake the bag. After a few seconds your meat would be fully covered in seasoning and ready to cook. Interestingly, this makes me think of our callings. You know, the things God has purposed us to do in this life. I think many of us have the assumption that it's going to feel right all the time.

Feelings are fleeting and have a tendency to lead people astray from momentary discomfort. There are ordained marriages that have fallen apart because there was a season of uncomfortability. It didn't feel right so therefore it must not have been right. This, of course, is far from true.

If comfort is a necessary determinant for recognizing an assignment, then we all would be lost. I don't remember there being a love seat on the cross. In Jesus's most agonizing moment he was right where he was supposed to be, fulfilling the calling on his life on the cross.

Contrary to popular belief he was not excited about it. We learn of his mental struggles and stress at Gethsemane when he asked for there to be another way. He hoped there was some other way in which our souls could be saved. But in the end he obeyed, and in his uncomfortability, we find comfort in the Father's arms. He was so stressed getting ready to be crucified that the capillaries in his sweat glands burst, and he sweat blood. It's obvious that none of us will endure what Christ endured. But we will suffer our own discomforts to serve the Lord. Maybe you are waiting to feel ready. What if that feeling never comes but God is still calling you to it. We depend on our feelings too much. That's why the previous example made sense to me. It's time for you to Shake 'n Bake. In other words do it scared. Do it shaking but keep cooking. Do it when you'd rather do something else. Do what he called you to, when you don't agree.

One of the funniest movies you will see is *Talladega Nights: The Ballad of Ricky Bobby*. It stars Will Ferrell and John C. Reilly. The only movie they've done that's funnier is *Step Brothers*. But in this movie they play two NASCAR racers who are on the same team. They are a phenomenal duo on the track. But the hilarious thing about their friendship is that to work themselves up for any situation they say "Shake 'n Bake" at each other. One says "Shake" while the other responds by saying, "n Bake." It really doesn't make sense, which they both acknowledge. But for some reason it works. It gets them going.

Saying it before you move doesn't make sense. But it works. I know this seems hilariously out of place but try it the next time you feel nervous before you go after what God told you to do. Say "Shake 'n Bake" and see how it affects your thought process. It doesn't make sense. You can't see why God chose you for this. You don't know why he desires for you to do this. But one of my newly found phrases that makes me laugh is "Let him cook." This is usually said when you hear someone spitting facts. I would explain what spitting facts means but I'm sure you can catch the colloquialism. Let it get you going. If anything at least you will get a good laugh out of it.

This next little bit may hurt a little so brace yourself for a moment. It's not my intent but it is necessary in my opinion. There is an unfortunate epidemic of false humility lurking through God's people these days. We feel God honors our disobedience if you do it in a humble presentation. I can see your eyebrows furrowing, reading this, preparing yourself to say, "What you talking 'bout, Willis?" I hear people say all the time, "Oh I'm a behind-the-scenes person." Yet you know God has called you to the stage. But here's where the rubber meets the road. False humility is telling God where you are comfortable serving and thinking it's ok because at least you are still serving. False humility is thinking that bargaining with God is possible —no matter how soft-spoken you are, no matter how meek you look. You can wrap poo in Christmas wrap with a bow or in newspapers. When it's unwrapped it's still the same thing.

Food for Thought:
    If God tells you that you are meant to be in the front, then humility is obediently on the stage, not behind the curtain. Humility is rarely where we want it to be, but it is always where God wants us to be.

I get it though. Like me, there are a lot of shy, nervous, and stage fright-filled individuals who think God is honoring their disobedient retreat from the limelight. Pause for a moment. Breathe ... I know that last statement may have been a little rough. This isn't for everybody but maybe it's specifically for you. I've been there. Actually not been ... I am there. This book is an obedience moment, not a move of my own. Honestly I was comfortable posting statuses on my Facebook page and enjoying the few hundred who liked it. Pro football Hall of Famer, Shannon Sharpe, once said that "comfortable is a great place to be, but nothing grows there.[1]" Do what he called you to do, even when you don't agree.

When God calls you to bigger he does not wait for your confidence or comfort level to match the size of the assignment. In other words we respond with respect to our insecurities. God does not. We respond with respect to our fears. God does not. The Word says he has not given us the spirit of fear. So he does not respect what he didn't give. But he does expect us to function through that mental foreign invader and show up.

I've been teaching God's Word for twenty plus years. I've spoken in front of thousands. I've also spoken in front of just a few people in an intimate setting. In both situations I'm almost always nervous before speaking. I'm afraid I'll say the wrong thing. I'm nervous I may slip up and get too excited and curse by accident. Kickstand right there for a moment will you. I have a cursing problem that God is still working on me with. Keeping it one hundred percent with you. I don't think I'm assisting him in the work though. For those that needed me to be perfect or at least cookie cutter to read this, sorry about that. I'm not your normal believer I guess. Actually, I am. I'm just not afraid to tell you my struggles.

Now let me get back to the point of this entry before my soapbox gets pulled out. If you truly believe God is all-powerful, since when are your flaws insurmountable? We love to say, "I can do all things through Jesus Christ who strengthens me." Well that includes the things he called you to that scare you. Remember, it's ok to Shake 'n Bake.

Let the nerves hit you. Feel the fear, because you are human. But today I declare in the name of Jesus that you will no longer let the fear be your master. Whoa, wait now, Dez, what do you mean, master? Fear is not my master. You sure? You will know a slave's owner by who they serve. If fear has directed your path and commanded you stand down ... and you obeyed, then it is your master.

It is not wrong to feel fear. It's wrong to obey it. Don't get me wrong as they say ... "Rome wasn't built in a day." Conquering fear is often progressive. But how do you eat a whole elephant? You start with one bite.

Find your first bite. Start writing the intro to the play. Lay out the blueprint for the business. Sure, you don't have the money or the resources, but give God something to respond to. I once led a band called Dez & The Future. I had never started my own band before. I could barely snap to cue my singers to sing. I rarely could get the timing right. I just knew it was what I was meant to do. So I invited people, in fear. I didn't even have a band, but I did the possible and left the impossible to God.

Fast forward to years later and some definite bumps and bruises. I had up to six backup singers, a band, and three sold-out concerts. How? God. I had nothing. But he met me at my faith move. He desires to meet you at your faith move. If you do the possible by showing up, he'll work through you. You may have done what I've done. I used to think God would need me to do everything. But that's not true. God is simply saying show up and I'll handle the rest. I stood on every stage of our concerts wondering how in the world all of this happened. Show up where he tells you to show up and watch him work.

Food for Thought:
    Give God room to show you that he's God.

In my experience people who are called to an assignment are often the opposite of that assignment. Not in all situations of course, but in many I've seen. For example Moses was called to speak to Pharaoh but he had a speech impediment. Even Jesus was called to draw all men to him but Isaiah 53:2 says, "He had no beauty or majesty to attract us to him, nothing in his appearance that we should desire him.[2]"

What if your anointing and your natural personality are complete opposites? What if you are naturally quiet but your calling needs you to talk? My wife and I laugh when people assume they can tell our personalities. We are often active in our gifts when people see us so they think it's how we are. I'm very expressive and often jovial when I teach and counsel, so people often think I'm like that all the time. But in truth I'm quiet and to myself.

On the other hand, my wife is often in business mode around people and a straight shooter. She has a gift for marketing, branding, and organization as a Certified Meeting Professional so people assume she's serious. But out of the two of us, she's the one with the most personality. You may be stalling your assignment because who you are doesn't seem to match up with your assignment. Let me let you in on a little secret—they weren't meant to match.

What he's called you to will make an impact that will be a big deal in his people's lives. We often have the same flaw that God's former choir director, Lucifer, had ... pride. We have a tendency to forget who's working through us. We will see the response of our peers and take credit without realizing it.

The offset of doing what doesn't match you allows for a beautiful phrase that keeps us humble, "I know that wasn't nothing but God" (excuse the grammar, but we have to keep the vernacular genuine to the culture). Being active in an anointing that doesn't match you makes staying humble easier. You know it was nothing but him because you don't even function naturally like that. That's why it's supernatural. It supersedes your natural to superimpose his nature on us. You don't even talk like that. That was nothing but the Holy Spirit. Stop denouncing your vocal anointing, quiet ones. It's the opposites that keep you connected and dependent on God. Get up there. Let's go. Shake ... (come on you know you want to say it.)

CHAPTER THIRTEEN
Relationships and Sex

I'm writing this entry on our seventh wedding anniversary. It's during some downtime for both of us. We came to San Diego, California for a week and visited family. I often feel sorry for those who don't give their marriage more than a couple of years. This next sentence may hurt a little but stay with me. Maybe you didn't give yourself enough time to realize that you were the problem in your marriage. I often hear people say they pray for God to change their spouse. It's often an unfinished prayer. I get it. I tried it, only to realize that I needed just as much change. Maybe even more.

I've watched people try to out-succeed their past. I've done it. We say, "Look, I'm successful. See that proves my past didn't effect me." But trauma can create an insatiable drive that everyone benefits from except you. When people benefit from your trauma they never find a reason for you to address it. This may seem different from most anniversary conversations. But I'm grateful ... grateful for the years to see me. Marriage isn't what you dreamed, it's what he ordained. Give it enough time to outgrow your assumed fantasy, to become your ecstasy. Someone's good development takes struggle to get there. A good marriage is no different.

She's softer than me. I didn't even know I was hard. She sees the world with an eye that I didn't know existed. Her heart hasn't hurt like mine has so she shows me some scars. I think we married people paint a picture that fools singles into thinking the potter's molding is only for your spouse. But the molding goes both ways. I've noticed over time that the people who often need the biggest change, complain the most about their spouse not changing.

These days entertainment has given a view of relationships that hinders real connection. Intimacy never starts with sex. It should end in sex after all covenants are met. Sex is the confirmation of the establishment of a relationship, not a practice run to see if it's worth a relationship. I seek only to establish some truths and this might feel rough, so hold on.

Good relationships usually require good character. There are outliers though. But here's where culture and faith collide. Men do not seek self-awareness for internal growth. They chase the dollar because it has now become the qualification for attraction. It is also confirmed in the word of many ladies who say they need to be paid to play. It's a transactional connection that appears one way, but is another.

Women do not seek awareness for internal growth as well. Many chase the exposure and changes of the body because it has become the qualifications for attraction. It's also confirmed in the words of men. It's a lustful connection that appears one way but is another. We would do well to ask people who've been in those situations for some years how it turned out. Often both sides are left lonely in the end.

Food for Thought:
Love without God is just lust in sheep's clothing.

Don't get me wrong. Physical attraction is a real thing. We all have eyes and preferences to the physical form of the opposite sex. The evidence of financial stability is also to be understood before entering into a relationship. The only issue is that now these two factors have become the only requirements for a "good relationship." Intimacy is so much more. I watched an interview of a woman, and they asked her if she was married. She lit up in her response and cheerfully said, "Yes."

They then asked, "Is he happy?" She was so caught off guard that she said, "That's a weird question." By the end of the interview it was obvious she had never thought of his happiness.

How often will the person you are with, think of your happiness? Transactional and lustful relationships will never care as much as they appear. They are receptive relationships, not reciprocal. Would they care or know what to say if you are having a bad day? Sex is not the answer to all issues. Some might have a thing to say about that last sentence, but let the relationship last a little longer. There is a honeymoon stage of sexual relationships that feels like they will last forever. But they drop off when it's no longer the answer.

Since we are on the subject, let's address one thing about sex. The bed is an interaction of three. It is the engagement of two people under the authority of one spirit. Sex after marriage is in the will of God ... therefore, it is under his authority. Here's where it gets dicey. Sex before marriage is the will of Satan ... therefore, it is under his authority.

Indicators for the doubters—sex with or without God will always confirm what the relationship is. It is confirmation, not recreation. Playing with a knife doesn't stop the knife from being dangerous. Fire never considers your playful nature before burning you. Maturity is a requirement for certain things no matter how tempting they are. Sex is not a playful sandbox. It's a serious commitment that many assume has no consequences. It's hard to hear but it also paints a different picture as to why God desired for us not to participate in sex prior to marriage.

Once I took some firewood with me while teaching young adults. I placed the firewood in the middle of everyone. I then grabbed a lighter and walked toward the wood. You could feel the nerves in the room. The gasps and energy amongst the young adults was a mix of fear and uneasiness. I asked if it was a good idea to light this flammable wood in this church. The overwhelming response was, "No!" I asked why it wasn't and why were they so nervous. They yelled answers. It could spread and burn the church down. You could get burned. It's dangerous. I wanted to know why it was dangerous. Why would they create firewood if it was so dangerous? The issue is not the fire, it's where it was placed.

In a fireplace, the firewood warms the room. It provides protection from the cold. In a stove it can even cook for you. But it's all about the placement. What was meant to bless you can burn everything down because it's in the wrong place. The Bible speaks of the want for sex like a burning desire. Before you listen to that desire, ask yourself what you could be burning down because it's out of place.

I can't judge anyone as I embark on great sex in my marriage. I know that last sentence may make a few people uncomfortable to say. But why is it a taboo subject. It shouldn't be. Today I'm attacking that nonsense. Sex in God's will is tremendous. It's not stale, and it's beautiful. There is something to look forward to if you wait. Even if you've experienced it already, give your body to God and watch him blow your mind when it's done the right way. The guilt after the act, outside of God is too heavy of a burden to bear. It's a struggle, but let me be your testimony that it's worth waiting.

CHAPTER FOURTEEN
Cartwheel Faith

I once heard a preacher tell a crazy story about faith. She was getting ready to preach and planned to wear a dress. In a change of plans God told her to wear leggings. She said, "I'm not doing that," but after a while she ended up obeying God. As she was before the people preaching, God said, "Do a cartwheel." Of course this didn't make any sense to her but she listened. In obedience she did the cartwheel. Immediately, a family stood up and said, "God is real!" She then said to the family, "Come up and tell us what's going on." The man told her that he was an atheist, well until now, and before service he prayed to whomever he thought might be God. He said, "If you are God, have the preacher to do a cartwheel."

Since that day he has been on fire for God and has since brought a multitude to Christ. Why is this important to you? First, God is not afraid to meet you where you are. If you are bold enough to pray it, he is bold enough to respond to it. In the Bible there was a man named Gideon. He was a great man who was told by God that he would lead his people to victory. But Gideon, like us, was human and fearful. The Israelites were being approached by opposition, and God had given Gideon authority to galvanize the army. However he was still afraid.

Food for Thought:
        There comes a time in your life where God may ask you to

do something that doesn't make sense to you. He may give no explanation but you know he has assigned you to do it. Never wait for the explanation. It making sense is not a requirement before being obedient.

In this case the preacher was told to do a cartwheel in front of a whole crowd and had no idea what was on the other side of her obedience. Too often God gives us assignments without understanding to allow faith through obedience to create a miracle.

What has God called you to do that you still don't understand? I've learned one thing that has given me a stomach full of humility. My understanding of what God wants to do through me, is not a requirement for me to be assigned. In other words, God does not have to consult with me before he sends a command down. Some of the greatest impacts in this life can be from something that doesn't make sense, but it resonates with people. How much sense does it make for a peaceful white man with an afro to create a TV program where he sits and paints scenery for half an hour? Nobody's going to watch that. Well they did. Bob Ross had us all mesmerized as he painted and talked to us about life, with a soft voice. His show, *The Joy of Painting*, aired for eleven years. In my opinion, he painted the same wilderness scenery over and over again, and we couldn't get enough.

Food for Thought:
You don't have to know how it'll work to start working.

This next example makes me laugh when I think about it, but it's true. I was in the car with my wife, and we were listening to an R&B station. "Pony" by Genuine came on. We both jumped up and prepared ourselves to sing the lyrics as if we had been his backup singers. As I listened to the lyrics, I wondered how the idea for this song came about. Who walked in the room and said, "Hey man, I got it. We'll have a grown man tell the women I want you to ride my pony." How crazy is that? But every new thing is crazy until it works.

That song went on to be his breakout single and hit #1 on the Billboard Hot R&B Singles chart. What crazy idea are you sitting on? You never know what is attached to your assignment. The preacher had no idea what that cartwheel would do. One cartwheel later and now there's a man on fire for God, leading people to Christ. What's your cartwheel?

The Bible speaks of a master and his three servants. He gave one five bags of gold. He gave another two bags of gold, and he gave the last servant only one bag of gold. Then he left them. When he returned, the one with the five had five more bags because he put his money to work. The second did the same and had doubled his as well. But the third servant buried his bag. When he had nothing to show, his master was displeased.

In the King James Translation of the Bible the bags of gold are called talents. It's such an intriguing thing to then ask, but are you the third servant? Are you the one who, instead of putting it in the world, you buried your talent? I wonder how many talents are buried in the sand of our doubts and fears. How many talents are covered in dirt because we can't see how it would work out? Your talent has a double portion waiting to bless the kingdom. But your opinion of said talent has it under soil instead of being invested in the marketplace to bless God's people.

God gave me an example to help me understand why my talents were not subject to my opinion. He reminded me when I was outside as a kid and I couldn't go inside to drink so I grabbed the water hose. He said the hose was necessary to get the water from the faucet. But what I didn't notice is that the hose gave water but rarely got water on me. The hose had water coming through it but rarely did the water splash back onto it.

It then dawned on me—you may not be as impressed as those being blessed from your talent because they are the kids, you are the hose, and God is the faucet. You may not understand because your job is to give your talent, not necessarily to receive your talent. You may not see it but maybe your talent isn't for your eyes. That's why you have to do it scared. Do it without feeling fully prepared when you've done the best you can. You may never be able to drink from the talents God has given you. But that does not give you the right to bend the hose. (For those who don't know, as we drank from the hose, if you were passing the hose to someone else you bent it to stop the water from coming out to save water.)

A lack of faith is us bending the hose. God never cuts off the faucet but we let our doubts cut off the water. If the faucet is open let your talent flow whether you understand it or not. The Word says our gift shall make room for us. It doesn't say we will understand how it makes room. Moral to the story? You never know what God is doing when he tells you to do something. But still do it. That crazy thing may be the one thing other people think makes sense. What's crazy to you may be ordained by God.

Here's a side note for you. You are reading my unearthed talent. For years people have been telling me to write a book and I felt ill-equipped to do so. I still do to a great degree, but you are reading the talent I was afraid to put into the marketplace. I'm writing this with no money and without a job. I'm writing from a place where God said, "There's enough in you." I'm writing from perceived lack. But my hope is stayed on the fact that Jesus was right. There is more in me.

So if I'm writing from this perspective, imagine what you can do. <u>There's more in you, even if there's nothing around you.</u> Don't wait for anybody to notice your talents. The only eyes that matter are God's. Notice that I didn't include your eyes. You may not see what God sees so trust his. Sometimes our eyes betray us. Pray this prayer.

God, open my eyes to what you see and blind me to the things I see. Block out my need to understand. Help me to trust you with the faith of a toddler to a father. Help me leap without seeing the bottom of the cliff. I rest my faith in you knowing when I don't. Amen.

One more thing about this topic—just because it wouldn't work for you doesn't mean it wouldn't work. You are just the vessel, not the receiver. We spoke about the hose not getting wet. That cartwheel did nothing for the preacher. Matter of fact it might've even been embarrassing. She was obedient to a command that had nothing for her. It didn't make sense because she couldn't see the point.

Your gift is not for your entertainment. It may not even bring you comfort. Stop looking for something out of what you give. It's for the masses, not you. Sometimes you will get a few drops of enjoying it, but most times you'll stay dry while others are drenched. You will be blessed by somebody else's gift, not yours. Still give it. That may be the only way it makes sense.

Have you ever seen somebody do something amazing and then they say stuff like, "Oh it wasn't that serious." It didn't make sense because you thought it was awesome. They don't get it because they don't get it. Read it again. They don't get it because they don't receive it. They are the giver, not the receiver. So let me slide your name in there.

Repeat after me:
I don't get it, because I don't receive it. But I don't need to understand it, to believe it. So I'll give it because people need it, just so everyone including myself, can leave blessed.

(In my Southern accent) Now go on and do it.

CHAPTER FIFTEEN
Caught in the Bushes

I have recently joined a new church called The Citadel in Jacksonville, Florida. Our pastor is Bishop Terry Hill Jr. In my opinion he's one of the best three biblical teachers in the city. I love Sunday service but my favorite service is Tuesday night Bible study. One particular week Bishop was out of town, so I had no intention of going. Yeah I know, that's messed up, but I can't lie about it.

In my eyes, if he ain't teaching then I ain't going. However, Bishop just had a meeting with all the leaders saying that he expected all of us to be at the mid-week services. I'm not gonna lie—that rebellious spirit was rising like the sun at first light. But something said go. Reluctantly I went. What I didn't know was that my brother from another mother (like Mel Gibson and Danny Glover) was teaching. Please excuse my *Lethal Weapon* reference.

I've known my "brother," Elder Marvin McQueen II, since we both worked at Communities In Schools years ago. He has always been as we African Americans like to say "good people." He was getting ready to teach about forgiveness, and I had no idea the greatness that was coming. He taught an amazing lesson that left me happy I went. One particular example he used led me to research. He spoke briefly about how Africans caught baboons. I looked it up, and here is what I found.

Baboons are protective of their sources of water in the Kalahari

Desert, but tribesmen over the years have figured out a clever way to get them to give up their locations. The men will dig a slender hole in an ant hill. He will then put melon seeds in it. Before he does all of this he makes sure a baboon is watching from afar. The baboon doesn't trust the man but he is still curious about what's in the hole. Once the seeds are in the hole the man walks away to watch. While he is away the baboon approaches the hole because it has to know what's in it. It reaches in to grab a handful but gets his hand stuck in the slender hole.

Eventually the baboon's arm becomes the chain to his own trap. If he would just let go, he could be free. But he doesn't want to let go of the melon seeds. What he's holding on to makes it insurmountable to escape.

Let me put a pin in that for just a second. What are you holding on to that you feel you have the right to hold on to? What offense has you so hurt that you refuse to let it go? I've been offended by people and held on to the offense for years. I've held on to it to the point that if anyone did or said anything that was close to what happened I went off or just immediately shut down. I've held grudges like I had the offenders on a chained rope and I had no intentions of releasing them. My thoughts had been if they apologized correctly I would forgive their offense and release them. But here's a truth that may bother some people. There is rarely an apology that fully suffices for an old offense. They can say the words and pain could still be there. I've even heard people say after an apology, "No that isn't enough. I need you to hurt like I was hurt."

Now back to our story … as soon as the man sees the baboon is caught he rushes to the hole. Of course the baboon is frantic but because he won't let go, he sees no way of escape. His hold has a hold on him. That right there is worth pausing for a second and thinking.

The man puts a rope around the baboon's neck and ties it to a tree. Once tied up, the man puts salt rocks on the ground next to the baboon. This is a favorite treat to baboons. As the baboon eats the salt rocks, it is so enamored that it forgets it's tied up while eating. But what the baboon is unaware of is the fact that while he's enjoying the snack, it's creating an insatiable thirst within. All through the night that thirst for water torments the baboon. It's all it can think about. It could care less about protecting its stuff, it just needs to quench the thirst. The next morning the man goes to the tree knowing, at this point, the thirst is so bad the baboon won't care who follows him. He releases the baboon, knowing it only has one destination in mind. He follows it closely until it reaches the secret watering hole. What was worth protecting changed in the desperation of a created thirst that could have been avoided if there had been an initial release.

I have realized that oftentimes people don't release offenses because we don't realize all we give up just to hold on to something that gives us some sense of control. We feel that releasing that person comes at surrendering what they did. But it's surrendering what you are.

American pastor, T.D. Jakes, once said[1], "Forgiveness does not exonerate the perpetrator. Forgiveness liberates the victim." That sounds good but was never enough for me to fully let go. I know that may not be for all of us but I needed more. I've been hurt in ways that weren't my fault and to release people from their offense seemed almost as unbearable as the offense. But I got tired of being a baboon. The melon seeds of unforgiveness were not rewarding enough to suffice the watering hole of joy and peace. I didn't realize how much of my treasure I was leading the enemy to, then wondering why it was tainted. Unforgiveness seems small but it has huge ramifications.

The greatest example of love was Jesus Christ dying on the cross for our sins. But why did he die on the cross for us? Here is a perspective you may have never considered. Jesus is also referred to as the second Adam. The first Adam, also the first sinless man, caused the break from God. That break could only be rectified by another sinless man.

In eating the forbidden fruit we were condemned to a separation from God. We had committed an offense that we alone could never atone for. We had offended God in a way that was wrong on another level. It removed us from Eden and his presence.

When Jesus came he endured the cross to atone for our offense. His whole purpose was to ensure our forgiveness and align us back with God. The greatest act of love was all about forgiveness. The greatest gift to man was rooted in forgiveness. This gives us a different perspective of love. This act speaks volumes to the motivation of love. We talk about how much God loves us, but many of us acknowledge his love on how much he forgives us on a daily basis.

Forgiveness is often the subconscious evidence to us that God loves us. In spite of our continual falls he still loves us. His love and grace are the evidence. In my personal opinion it looks like love in its purest form.

If forgiveness is one of God's greatest pieces of evidence of love, then unforgiveness must be the opposite. If forgiveness is love then unforgiveness is something we may not want to admit. Hatred opens the door to everything that is not God, and temporary desires create thirsts that lead the devil to our treasures.

You may think your unforgiveness isn't doing much but as you hold on to the melon seeds, you give the devil room to tie you up. Then he offers treats. Sin enters easily. For the moment it satisfies you. Instead of being the salt of the world, you consume the salt of the worldly. And the devil has mastered the greatest pull to get someone to sin—put unforgiveness in their heart. From then on they'll hold themselves in place to tie down.

You'd be surprised at how much you are falling into simply because you won't forgive those who hurt you. Instead, you try chopping down the stalk of a tree, not realizing the problem is the root. Many times you can't see the roots, or better yet, you refuse to see the roots. If you can't see them, you can't remove the issue.

Many of us struggle with issues because one main issue isn't addressed. There are medical problems that are a direct result of other things in the body.

But it hurts too much to address. No, my friend you are hurting too much not to address it.

You won't let go, and you are wondering why you are in a hole feeling like a baboon.

CHAPTER SIXTEEN
Mountain Top

Everybody wants to get to the top of the mountain until they realize it's cold and hard to breathe up there. There is ice at the top of mountains in Africa, but the valley at the bottom is warm.

The tallest mountain in the world is Mount Everest, standing at 29,029 feet above sea level. For this reason many climbers have sought to conquer the rugged terrain. Unfortunately, there are many who were unable to finish. There are also many who have drawn their last breath in the attempt. It is said that there are over 200 bodies still on the mountain of fallen climbers. This is not a conversation to never climb, rather an attempt to make sure you are climbing the right mountain.

There are 1,187,049 mountains in the world. Not everybody was meant to climb Mount Everest. But there are some who climbed Everest but would perish on the mountain others were meant to climb. Based on the way we are taught, Mount Everest seems like the only choice, being the tallest. It's bragging rights, the best. But is it?

Food for Thought:

If everyone seeks one climb, there will never be room for everyone at the top. So which mountain is yours and which mountain is the distraction? Which climb is the dream and which climb is the proof?

We champion those with strong drives to do things. We respect their fervor. But we never ask where the drive came from. Some of us are driven by the desire to prove. The "they'll see" mentality has led many to the wrong mountain. Trying to show people your worth is a quick way to see your purpose perish. You'll see it take its last breath on the side of a climb not meant for you. You are worthy whether they see it or not.

Sometimes God camouflages our anointing to blend in with the crowd. It's necessary because those we try to prove ourselves to would misuse us. Simply put, sometimes they can't see you because God doesn't want them to.

American rapper, Lil' Kim, once said[1], "The key to life is money, power, and respect." But I dare say that if you use that key to unlock your purpose, the door won't open. It's not that the key won't work on other locks. However, your door will never open if that's your focus.

We as a society are short-changed by the promises of consumer ideologies. We are taught that the more you get, the more you are. In reality, the more someone has consumed, the more they forget who created them. We are often deceived to think the enemy desires for us to be penniless. He could care less about your poverty or your wealth. He cares about your separation from God. The more you are separate, the less of a threat you are.

On the opposite end there are those so distracted by their desire to have, that they separate themselves from God in the pursuit of keeping up with the Joneses. We all have a genuine purpose, but we also have tendencies to create purposes that fulfill hidden agendas cloaked in dreams. Simple question—what is God's dream for your life? Have you asked? Or is the "money god" still providing you with the dreams you desire?

American rapper, Biggie Smalls, once said[2], "More money, more problems." That seems impossible to imagine for those without it. But what do you do when what you assume to be the answer becomes more of the problem. Lottery winners have often gone broke. Professional athletes have often gone broke. Money is a powerful distraction without the provision of God.

Food for Thought:
If God provides all your needs then why is money the thing you covet the most?

1 Timothy 6:10[3] says that "Love for money causes all kinds of evil."

To be clear money is not evil. It is not evil to be wealthy. But the actual "love" of money is the root of all evil. I like the way the Message Bible puts it:

"But if it's only money these leaders are after, they'll self-destruct in no time. Lust for money brings trouble and nothing but trouble. Going down that path, some lose their footing in the faith completely and live to regret it bitterly ever after."
(*The MESSAGE*, 1 Timothy 6:9-10)[4]

So what does money provide? Money provides tangible access. With enough, it can give the perception of being able to do anything, buy anything, and be anything. Without the guidance of God it champions as a false provider. In short, the love of access without God is the root of all evil.

"Again I tell you, it is hard for a camel to go through the eye of a needle. But it is even harder for someone who is rich to enter the kingdom of God."
(*New International Reader's Version*, Matthew 19:24)[5]

How can I tell you that you need Jesus when, in your eyes, you have everything you need and want? It's hard to interpret "need" if you've never experienced it. It's hard to explain starving to a man who's never experienced hunger. But there is a deeper need that extends beyond what money can buy. It's just hard to see that you need joy, when you can keep purchasing temporary happiness. It's hard to see you need love if wealth offers you conditional loyalty.

Job in the Bible was a wealthy and beloved man until he went broke. As a result everyone left.

You can go through life and have an occupation that gains you money, power, and even fame outside of the will of God. Artists with albums boast about all of the things opposite to God. They can confuse people by saying, "First I'd like to thank God for this award." The devil gives out awards all the time.

When Jesus was being tempted, the devil offered him the world. I'm sure he would've given it to Jesus, too, just so he wouldn't have to worry about him fulfilling his purpose. The scariest thing to the devil is to submit to God's purpose without an expectation of personal greatness—God, I will be what you want me to be whether it's what I want or not. We misuse a popular scripture all the time.

"I can do all things through Christ which strengtheneth me."
(Philippians 4:13 KJV)[6]

The key word is "through." The "things" must be approved first before attempted. It is not a ticket to do what we want. In actuality it was a declaration of endurance. I can endure these things that oppose me through the strength of Christ.

"What good is it if someone gains the whole world but loses their soul?"
(*New International Reader's Version*, Mark 8:36)[7]

You can gain the whole world and what it has to offer without being in the will of God. You can have the riches you desire outside of his will. But will it be worth it? In this description it is easy to believe that, in God's eyes, your soul is way more valuable than the world. Even if you can't see that, go with God's value scale.

How would one gain the whole world? What would be the avenues for gaining? If those avenues are the keys to worldly access, then maybe they aren't the keys to peace. It doesn't matter how much money you have. You can't buy the fruits of the spirit.

Food for Thought:
You can't buy God's presence. But you can buy your distraction and you can't afford the misdirection.

Money has us confused as to who is blessed and who isn't. Some people you envy are living under a curse with a nice bank account. Not all, but some. You can always tell because for some reason they can't stand you. They can't seem to put their finger on it, but for some reason, they can't stomach your presence. It's because no matter how much they buy and own, they can't seem to afford the smile you have in storms. The annoying part is that you seem to have it with less.

The devil owns a lot of people because their loyalty was bought. But you came at a cost he couldn't pay. Pick your head up. You are a wealthy kid in a foreign land. Your Father may not have chosen to send your riches over here because he has no intentions for you to stay over here. If the money comes, fine. If it doesn't, fine. Never let it be the determining factor as to whether you are blessed or not. Sometimes blessed is just being able to sleep at night, knowing the Lord is on your side.

CHAPTER SEVENTEEN
Bucket

In my early years of pursuing a music career I had a group called Dez & The Future. I know I'm probably being biased but we were really good. I had three sold-out concerts and a decent reputation around the city. After a while things fell apart. Certain members had to be replaced over time. It became a problem I was frustrated with. I just didn't understand.

I was meticulous with the vocal arrangements to keep the attention of the members and crowds. I even worked hard to create our own sound. But in the end, we still suffered from inconsistencies.

We practiced all the time. But that was the issue. I was so focused on making sure we got the songs on point, I was critiquing each practice trying to make sure we were perfect. It literally became the only thing we did. There were little to no performances. I barely took invitations to go anywhere, because I knew we weren't ready. Members were ready to perform, and I just knew we needed more practice. There was always something to tweak in the songs, but performers want to perform.

The practice had to be leading up to something but it never was. Many left and had to be replaced. The truth is there was no way of practicing out of the human dynamic. I was saying we needed practice because I was afraid to present. That mindset became a problem in the dream being fulfilled.

In December of 1989 a young and broke Will Smith was invited to a party with multiple celebrities and other affluent individuals. Quincy Jones, one of the greatest composers of all time, walked up to Will and said, "Here is a script for a new show. Brandon Tartikoff, the head of NBC, is here. I want you to take ten minutes to study the script. Then I want you to be ready to present.[1]"

Of course Will was shocked, and in desperation, he requested a week to prepare for the audition. Quincy responded by saying, "Ok, I can schedule a week from today, and you know what's going to happen. He's going to be booked. Then I can reschedule again, and he'll be booked again. Or you can take ten minutes right now and change your life forever."

During President Barack Obama's White House Correspondents' Dinner[2] he recalled a moment with his advisors. They asked if he had a bucket list. This to which he responded by saying, "No but I do have something that rhymes with it." He then appealed to the crowd by saying, "Take executive action on immigration ... bucket. New climate regulations ... bucket." The crowd roared in laughter, and it was understood where he was going. To that point, every topic he no longer deemed serious his response was ... bucket. It may have been serious before but now ... (shrug your shoulders) bucket.

When Quincy told Will that this was his moment, Will responded by saying something similar to President Obama. I believe he had an Eminem "Lose Yourself" moment. If you had one shot or one opportunity to seize everything you ever wanted, would you capture it or let it slip? The question at hand is what are you letting slip because you say you are not ready? There is a Chinese proverb that says, "Doing is better than talking on and on, stating one's own points."

The time for talk is over. It's time to launch.

Food for Thought:
    Perfectionism is a disease that stalls greatness.

Some of the corrections will come in the launch, not the preparation. **Perfection is never necessary for the beginning but it is achieved in the repetition of the execution.** The last show is always the best show of any production because it has worked out the on-stage kinks nobody could've expected. Sometimes you have to hit the stage a few times before you feel ready. You are talking too much, you have planned enough. You have prayed about it and got your answer. Now launch.

They say the word fear is an acronym for false evidence appearing real. You can't use false evidence in the case of your dream to prove your innocence. Fear will charge you every time. Please get that double entendre. You can't prove your inability to move by presenting your inexperience. It won't hold up because your evidence is presented in fear. You may be on the precipice of your big break in something you weren't expecting.

Will was a rapper, not an actor. He had no training. But he had an opportunity. He was pushed into a career he wasn't looking for, and in the launch, he got his training. James Avery who played the role of the beloved character Uncle Phil became Will's on-stage acting coach. Will gleaned from Avery and developed through watching his highly trained mentor on the set of *The Fresh Prince of Bel Air*. I honestly believe this on-screen training led to Will's amazing future of starring in multiple films. He eventually became more known for his acting than his music. Is this your moment, and are you letting it slip?

As I said before, my wife and I joined The Citadel Church of Jacksonville in 2024. We had previously been a part of another ministry within the city, but after much prayer, we realized it was time to leave. At our previous church I was certified in four areas of ministry and had nine years of ministry experience as a youth and young adult pastor. I wasn't necessarily trying to bring that up in our new church. I actually wanted to sit for a while. However, that was not the plan. We joined one week, and two weeks later I was on program to preside over a service.

Mentally I was a wreck. It was a new house, which meant a new way of doing things. I was afraid to mess up. Sure I was a minister but I was new. I made up my mind that I was going to ask to be removed from the service and allowed a few weeks to get accustomed to the way things are run. I told my wife about my decision, and to my astonishment, she didn't seem to agree. We then had a conversation that rocked me. She said, "These people know who you are. They recognize your experience and are responding accordingly. They are pushing for you to do all these things because they can see greatness in you." I was stunned. What stood out is that I saw myself in the moment.

Food for Thought:
Sometimes where you are meant to be and what you are meant to do will not wait on your belief in who you are to push you into what you've always been. (I know that's a mouth full, but if you slow it down it makes sense.)

Oftentimes those you are supposed to be around believe in you more than you believe in yourself. In those moments go with their belief and not yours. Go with the mindset, "God I believe but help my unbelief. " Sometimes being fully persuaded is an action that does not require you being fully convinced. Imposter's syndrome plagues the launching pad. But do it anyway. Don't wait to believe it. Just launch it. Move. Newton's Third Law states that for every action there is an equal and opposite reaction. Inactivity creates no opportunity for the reactions necessary for your elevation. Let the reactions of your actions create moments that could possibly change your life. Don't waste time stuck trying to figure out which way to go.

Food for Thought:
Make a decision, execute the decision, and if it's a failure at least now you know which way not to go. But you also now know

where to go.

I was invited to speak at this huge campus ministry conference called Campus Harvest. I was nervous because it was in an auditorium that held thousands of people, and it was jam packed. I just didn't want to mess up. I was sitting in the back, apparently looking crazy because this unassuming white brother with a bald head walked over to me. He asked, "Are you ok?" I responded by saying, "No, I'm nervous. I just don't want to mess up out there."

Now let me remind you, this is a huge conference with a bunch of deep people there. So my expectation was for him to respond with loving affirmations like "you got this" or "it'll be fine." But to my surprise he said something that changed my life. "You're not that big."

I looked over at him so quick I almost snapped my neck. Wait, what? He continued by saying, "Our issue is that we think that we are flawed beyond use, as if our flaws are insurmountable for God." He told me that I'm not so big of an issue that God can't do great work though me ... that even my bad decisions and failures will still work as long as I'm doing my best to serve the Lord's purpose for my life.

> "We know that in all things God works for the good of those who love him. He appointed them to be saved in keeping with his purpose."
>
> (Romans 8:28)[3]

That freed me, and I hope it frees you. God is great enough to know our flaws and still use us beyond them. Moses had a speech impediment, and God still used him to speak before Pharaoh. No matter the flaw, it's not big enough to halt what God wants to do through you. There's a quote that says, "A diamond with a flaw is better than a common stone that is perfect." So if it happens quicker than you expect, jump. If it happens in a way you don't expect, jump. If you are ready but don't want to do it out of fear, jump. If you feel like you are unprepared but it's your moment ... bucket and jump.

Dez Demps

CHAPTER EIGHTEEN
Unfun Forgiveness

Many times when we talk about forgiveness there is a victim mentality that clouds our ability to see the truth. I'm not saying this is true for all things but there is an area of discussion necessary for growth.

We don't have to discuss the rightfully dismissed people. But it's time to go back and forgive those who were right in their "offense." It is easy to avoid accountability when being a victim takes the blame away.

Imagine if The Father and Jesus were in heaven right now and they weren't on talking terms because Jesus was still mad over what he went through. Imagine Jesus saying, "How could you let me go through that?" There was a moment before the crucifixion where Jesus cried out to The Father. Drenched in his own sweat and blood he pleaded …

> "My Father, if it is possible, take this cup of suffering away from me. But let what you want be done, not what I want."
>
> (Matthew 26:39b)[1]

He said this multiple times to no response. He was also betrayed by a friend, deserted by others, beaten, whipped, and nailed to a cross. He even spoke on the cross in disbelief...

***

"Eli, Eli, lema sabachthani?" This means "My God, my God, why have you deserted me?"

(Matthew 27:46b)[2]

He didn't understand in his time of trials. He felt deserted. But at the end, after the resurrection, it was clear his struggles were necessary to save man and correct the broken covenant made by man. It was clear that no man would be worthy enough to do it and that without Jesus, man would forever be doomed to man's mistake in the garden. It was bigger than the pain. It was necessary for purpose. So when Jesus sat at the right hand of The Father there was no animosity. It was understood.

The victim mentality keeps us from understanding. You thought people turned their back on you. Now seeing the results, you know they were right in letting you go through what you went through. It's time to return to those who were right.

Being a victim corroded your good friend circle. Now you are surrounded by people you can't trust because you don't want to return to the person you could trust and say, "You were right." They were right that a person was no good for you. Now that the terrible relationship is over and the proof is in the outcome, go back and reconcile.

Wise and good friends are willing to lose a friend in order to tell them the truth. They knew you wouldn't like what they had to say and that they would probably lose a friendship. But they loved you enough to tell you when it would mean losing someone they loved. Good friends like that are hard to find.

Go back, apologize, and maybe listen the next time they have advice you don't like. They could be saving you from a trap you can't see. The Father was right to turn his back on Jesus on the cross. He was right to stay silent at Gethsemane. He was right not to interfere as Jesus was enduring necessary trials. Your parent was right to not save you this time. They were right to allow you to go through what you went through. You know it's true. Even you feel like you've matured. It's time to reconcile. They weren't wrong.

You may be thinking, "Yeah but I still don't like the way they said it." But were they right? Sometimes a harsh tone is a reflection of passionate fear and even love. They were afraid for you, and in their attempt to steer you right, it came off harsh. But again, were they right?

We also have a tendency to lean on someone's tone as our excuse to maintain our position as a victim. Perfection is a trait of The Lord, not man. Give grace to a bad tone but loving intention. Give the grace you want given to you. It's time to sit at the right hand of that friend or family member again. The storm is over, the lessons are learned. Don't let pride stop you from returning just because you don't want to tell a proven ally they were right.

CHAPTER NINETEEN
Dis-Located

Have you ever woken up angry with the blessing God gave you? You prayed for a job and God gave it to you, but you've had it for a few years and find yourself more and more angry with it. You prayed for God to bless you with a spouse and God gave them to you, but you find yourself more and more angry with them. It's not that you aren't blessed. It's that the blessings are really making you mad and you don't know why. You try not to be bothered but you can't seem to get through the day without finding something about whom or what God blessed you with, that doesn't bother you.

As a youth pastor I remember visiting one of my kids in the hospital. It was my second week of ministry and my second time going to the hospital to check on a youth that had been shot. Side note, Jacksonville Florida is a tough place for ministry. They don't call Duval County "The Bang 'Em" for no reason.

As I sat in the waiting area, I noticed this man standing across from me in his tank top. Now we all know hospitals are cold. I was confused because he was a slender man, so he had no personal insulation to keep him warm. I just so happened to look at his shoulder, and one looked totally different from the other. His right shoulder was significantly lower. For some reason he seemed cool about it and was talkative about the incident. I don't know why, but he decided to talk to me and tell me what happened. For some reason this happens to me a lot.

Long story short, he was trying to live out his old glory days playing sports and ended up throwing his shoulder out. But the funny part is he was making jokes about it the whole time. Nevertheless, I imagine his demeanor would change if I asked him to lift up his arm a little. I bet if someone barely moved his arm he would instantly yell in discomfort or even curse out of sheer pain. Now if his arm was in place, I could ask him to move his arm like usual and it wouldn't even bother him. He wouldn't care and would probably stay in his jovial demeanor. It was easy to see his natural character because even in obvious consistent pain, he still wanted to have fun. But painful dislocations tend to make us act out of character.

I woke up angry for no reason, and my wife was irritating to me out of nowhere. All I could do was think of all she had done in the past and all of our normal disagreements. Even her hello annoyed me because I was in a bad mood. Now the "old me" would have never considered myself to be the problem. I would've responded in my anger, and soon after an argument would erupt. But I asked, "Why am I so angry?" Then it dawned on me. I started reading my Bible every morning and this particular day I hadn't done that. So, my spirit was dislocated, and I was responding out of the discomfort of my spirit being drained.

Now don't get me wrong. I'm not suggesting you are a heathen if you don't read your Bible every morning. I just needed to because I was in a harder than normal season. My character was off because my connection was dislocated. After taking some time out with God it made the other parts of my life align, and in turn, I aligned better overall.

Food for Thought:
    Sometimes that bad attitude is not a personality trait as much as it is evidence of your dislocation.

We are not as autonomous as we think we are. God is the key component to our serenity. If we are the car, he is the gas. Without him we cannot move in our purpose. Without him we go nowhere and complain about being stagnant. He is the catalyst to motion and serenity. Without him we become sensitive to the slightest touch and snarl at those closest to us because it hurts to move.

You may be thinking, "Well, that's cool, Dez, but I read my Word and I'm still dealing." There will always be things in a Christian's life that we will have to deal with. But we don't have to lack peace. However, peace does not always mean comfortable. Jesus was once at the bottom of a boat asleep on a cushion while the waves rocked the boat. It was so bad the boat was taking in water. We often rush to the part where Jesus was woken up by the disciples and calmed the storm. But he slept through a storm. Maybe your storm isn't over because he's waiting for you to stop waiting for the storm to finish before you rest.

Food for Thought:
  Peace does not require your environment to be at peace.

I remember in my twenties when God told me he wanted me to jog on a regular basis. Candidly I must admit I can't stand jogging. It is the bane of my existence. That is, I hate running when I begin, but love it when I return home.

I've often tried to bargain with God by reading my Word and thinking that was enough. But trading a good thing for a God-thing is still disobedience. Now this is where it gets tough because many of us are used to taking the easy road and getting away with it. You are not slick enough where you can fool God. The repercussions of disobedience have ripples. It is not an isolated event. The ripples hit everything, not just the thing you missed.

Food for Thought:
  God is everywhere, but his blessings are not.

A lot of long-distance relationships struggle because the person you are with is not in your presence often. The physical distance often causes emotional distance in the relationship. It's the consistent presence of someone that makes the relationship easier. Not to say that some people haven't found a way to make it work, but for many it's tough. Many of us have a long-distance relationship with God. We are not often in his presence but claim to be in a relationship and wonder why it's so strained.

One thing that always makes me laugh is when my wife picks up certain sayings from me just from hanging around me. She even has picked up a few character traits. I've done the same with her. God's character is peace, love, serenity, etc. (I Corinthians 13:4-8)[1]. You pick up on those traits by just being around him.

Maybe the thing steering you to other thoughts and feelings is simply not being where he is. Maybe the uncomfortability is dislocation. You want peace? Ask yourself where you are supposed to be. Are you around the people and places you are supposed to be around? Are you in the right location? Being who you are but not where he wants you to be can change your character.

That man at the hospital's character was subject to the pain of his dislocation. At any moment he could go from Dr. Jekyll to Mr. Hyde based on who or what triggered his dislocation. He was naturally a fun guy but the pain created a new personality that didn't match his normal state. I wonder how well your natural personality is holding up being out of place. Maybe you are like me. I don't do well being far from God. It's time to get closer.

CHAPTER TWENTY
The Best Part

One of my favorite artists, H.E.R., has a song out that's called the "Best Part." It's a beautiful song that had the R&B world in a chokehold for weeks. Have you ever been watching your favorite movie, and someone started talking and you had to tell them, "Shh, this is the best part." Or you were watching a highlight replay in sports and you tell your friend who missed it, "Look, this is the best part." There are things right in front of us that we miss because it's not happening the way we expect it or when we should have been paying attention.

In the Bible a man by the name of David was anointed, in his youth, to be king. But his journey on the road to becoming king was no crystal staircase. If you pay attention to scripture, most of his story was recorded of him on his journey to becoming a king rather than being the king.

I believe even Jesus saw His tough journey leading to the cross and said to us, "Look, this is the best part." Too often we are so excited to get to the success that we miss the best part … the process. It was in the process that our story was written or even interesting.

In biopics you see the journey to what the person had to go through and what they put themselves through. At the end of the movie you see words on the screen that usually start like "and they went on to…," which is followed by a list of accolades. As much as the success is stabilizing and exciting, only the process is inspiring and uplifting.

What am I saying? Sit back, lay down, and enjoy the rocking of the boat. What you are allowing to trouble and keep you up is supposed to be helping you sleep like it did for Jesus. Stop trying to fast forward your turmoil, you are missing the best part. There are letdowns to life.

Every day is not going to go the way you expect it to go. You will be disappointed. You will endure struggle. American singer and songwriter, Frankie Beverly, said it best, "Joy and pain are like sunshine and rain.[1]" Some of the hardest moments of your life may produce some of the best character traits within you. Yes, last season bothered you but look who you are becoming. Look what the struggle is producing. You keep struggling with the same bench press long enough, eventually it's not a struggle because you got stronger.

But let's be honest. Accepting the moment when things don't go the way you want them to can be hard. You had an expectation and even pictured yourself with the person, place, or thing. It's hard to take a no that you really wanted to be a yes. You go through guilt for believing in it. You feel less of yourself and you feel discouraged.

I remember the early struggles of going through a time of turmoil. In my eyes, God had me in the waiting room a little too long for my blessing. I couldn't see my way out. I thought I would have been on my way out before then. Was I even supposed to be in this waiting room in the first place or was I waiting for nothing? It got depressing. I had never been there before, and I was starting to lose my faith in things turning out ok.

One day I just began to cry out to God in desperation. He responded with "3:16." I didn't understand it. I was expecting more. I knew he was referring to in John 3:16 [2]but I couldn't see the point. Most Christians know that scripture by heart. What does that have to do with this? I heard it for days and I responded in anger and confusion. Why are you telling me this? Until one day I just decided to read it in frustration.

"For God so loved the world that he gave his only begotten son that whosoever believes in him shall not perish" … then he said, "Stop."

I froze because I didn't see that coming. Without needing to ask, I knew what he was saying. In a simple phrase he said, "You shall not perish."

I was in the mist of turmoil, and God assured me that although I had not reached the finish line, I would not perish before I got there. Instantly, I felt a weight lifted in me. It became the peaceful reminder of my life.

Keeping it honest, I am not writing this book from an uplifted place. I'm still trusting and believing in what God has said but I'm currently not seeing it. You are reading the words of a man in real time who just received disappointing news about a lost opportunity that would've changed my life. I feared being this transparent in my writing but maybe it's necessary for you to read this.

I'm trusting God in a season where the fog is so dense, I can barely see my hand in front of my face. Maybe you feel this way. Maybe you are trying to trust him when you can't see, and have to trust that his eyes are so high that they see above the thing that blocks yours. I don't know. But what I do know is that where I can't see ahead of me, I have clear vision behind me.

I remember previous situations where he held me up in times of trouble. I remember times where I was almost gone—I mean literally almost un-alive by my own bad choices. The only thing holding me now is that I can't see where his new promises are going but I can see where his old promises have been. He's never let me down. I won't get too preachy because he has made me wait before, and that did frustrate me. But he has never let me endure defeat. All my life's giants have fallen with me only being armed with a flimsy slingshot and a trust in God.

In his old age King David once said, "I was young and now I am old, yet I have never seen the righteous forsaken" (Psalms 37:25)[3]. That gives me solace to sleep at the bottom in this boat while the storm is raging.

Interesting enough today it's raining outside my window. The downpour is so heavy, flood warnings are all over the city. I've been hearing raindrops sounding like white noise on the panels of my sliding door for hours. God has a way of making a metaphor come to light doesn't he. If you are like me in this season, I pray your days of waiting are filled with the peace of knowing the Lord will not allow you to perish and that he has not forsaken you. But as I am trying to do, I hope you do the same. Don't miss the best part. Storms never last forever, no matter how long they last.

CHAPTER TWENTY-ONE
Egairram

This one is for the married folk and those who hope to be married. If you do things before the timing, you could start a God-thing off incorrectly. You can be in the right thing the wrong way.

Imagine you are running track. Now there is the 100, 400, 800, 4x4, 4x8, etc. but you are a 400 runner, and you sign up for the 400 race. You get in the right lane and while everyone gets in their stance, you turn around because someone told you this would make you run better. When the gun fires you run in the same direction as everybody else but backwards. Everyone else smokes you, of course. Your quads hurt because they are not moving the way they were meant for maximum speed. You keep looking over your shoulder to see where you are going while trying not to stumble. Then when you realize the issue and try to turn around halfway through the race, you trip over your feet and fall mid-turn. You then get up off the ground and begin to run the right way.

The truth is you can be in the right race, in the right lane, and where you are supposed to be but not doing it the right way. You can be where you are supposed to be and not the way you are supposed to be there. This is how some marriages are. You are with the right person, in the right marriage, but started the wrong way.

We don't discuss this part of marriage because most of us start the race off backwards. We have sex before marriage. We move in together before marriage. We have kids on purpose. We marry people before God is done with them. We are too early or too late. Then when the consequences come, we compare ourselves to other couples and let our assumptions run wild because people aren't wearing their rough marital testimony on their foreheads.

Races themselves are hard enough. It takes endurance, focus, and steadfastness. But with a mantle that already holds weight, we add more weight and wonder why we are on the verge of crumbling. It's not the marriage's fault—it's the actions before that created calamity before the holy work could start.

Marriage is holy work no matter how we started. I think by now I may have ruffled some feathers, so let's be honest. Staying true to the parameters God placed for the "right way" is hard. How do you look at someone you love and not touch them in an unholy way? They are God-sent but they are sexy, too. Oh don't clutch your pearls now. American comedian and television host, Steve Harvey, said[1] it best. "If Christians ain't sexy then where all these little Christians keep coming from?"

It's a struggle to stick to the strict script God lays out for us. So as I talk, know that it's real but it doesn't remove the reality that the struggle is real. My hope is if we get in-depth with certain consequences, maybe it'll help cool the flame when things get hot and impatience almost reigns supreme.

Imagine driving in traffic, putting your car on cruise control, and jumping in the back for a nap. More than likely you won't even get to the back before you crash. Either way the crash is inevitable. But if it is a God-ordained car, there is no such thing as totaled. It can always be fixed.

Again, apart from abuse a marriage can always be fixed. But let God be the body shop. You can strive for greatness in the ministry of marriage. It takes work. It's just not heavy. It just takes beloved work. But the addition of disobedience creates calamity, which creates extra work, and we were only allotted a certain amount of energy to exert for a certain amount of work.

Many troubled marriages aren't in turmoil as much as they are in burnout. You are having to put out fires that were never meant to be lit and you are tired before you can get to the normal tasks. You think things like, "How do you want to talk about this, when we just had to handle that? How do you want to deal with the kids when we can't deal with each other?" It feels like you don't have enough. Therefore, you don't feel like enough. Instead of taking hold of your feelings about yourself, you project them onto your spouse and convince yourself that they aren't enough. However, the truth is you started out running backwards, and now that you are trying to turn it around, you fall flat because you tripped over yourself.

The Word says that in marriage two become one. So, when you trip over yourself you could be the right leg and your spouse could be the left. In a sense you are tripping over each other because one could be desiring to change before the other. If they need more time to change that does not mean quit. Pastor Michael Todd of Transformation Church in Tulsa, Oklahoma once spoke about dating in a way I had never heard. In short, he basically said that relationships before marriage taught us how to break up, not stay together. If we were agitated, we just broke up with the person. We became conditioned to move on when things got tough. But what God puts together let no man put asunder … including you.

Food for Thought:
>   If God hasn't given up on your marriage neither should you.

If he put you two together in matrimony, you do not have his permission to tear you two apart. It doesn't matter how you started it. Even if you finish last while watching others finish earlier, stay in it. You never know what type of "speed ups" God has along the way.

We often hear the virtues of love. But one of the most important ones we skip is "steadfastness" (1 Corinthians 13:4-7)[2]. Stay in there with God's choice. This is a promise not a prison, it's a season not a sentence. I know a few of you may have been wondering why this entry is called "Egairram." Some marriages start out backwards. But it will go forward by patiently rearranging the letters over time. Simple suggestion but the two letters that work well to start with your rearranging is the "M-E."

CHAPTER TWENTY-TWO
Oh Boy

This is going to be a very open and honest entry, so lock in ... I'm tired of writing this book. I want to move on to the next thing. I'm no longer as excited as I was when I first got the revelation to do it.

I've begun to critique old entries as I read back checking for errors. It doesn't seem as appealing as it did before. I honestly only have a few more chapters to write but something has set in. I don't know if I don't know what is going on. Read that last sentence one more time so you don't get thrown off by it. You read it? Ok, cool, let's move on. If you didn't, stop being disobedient, like me. Alright, let's move for real. I'm probably just stalling. I'm avoiding the inevitable. I'm afraid ... afraid to be the idiot who thought he was smart enough to write a book when he knows he doesn't enjoy reading. (Insert explicative word) I can't believe I'm getting choked up after saying that. I need a second.

(Fifteen minutes later) Ok, I'm back. I know you didn't experience what I just did, but I took a moment to gather myself and started writing again. This is probably the hardest entry for me to write. Vulnerability is honorable in thought, but terrible in experience. I despise this moment. I honestly don't even know if this chapter is a part of God's will. My hope is that I'm not just venting and there is something in all of this. I'm blind to purpose, while the struggle is in high definition.

Personally every time I read inspirational books I'm always reading up. I know authors don't mean to, and I definitely haven't read all the books in the world. But there always seems to be this condescending undertone of "I've arrived, get like me," in those books. The testimonies are always past tense and victorious. Even the failures wrap around to some triumphant superhuman push to victory. In an attempt to inspire they seem like a person we'll never become. But in short, they seem barely human.

Well it's hard to admit, but I'm having a real human moment right now. No I don't want you to be a part of it. I'm not enjoying it. But (insert explicative word) I'm here and I don't want to hide this part of the process from you. My mom once said, "You've accomplished a lot to be as young as you are." Excuse the example. I just said people love to tell stories about being in the "I've arrived column," but here I go on the humble brag—each project God had me on came with a crossroads moment. I don't know if I've ever talked about it out loud, but here we go. It's the point where you don't have the motivation to finish but you know you need to. It feels like dragging a "you-sized" bag of potatoes up a steep hill.

When I was a senior in high school it was something like "Senioritis." You're so close to finishing you don't want to do anything anymore. God is quieter here. He was talking real good at the beginning (of me writing this book), but at the end he seems very much on his Beyoncé concert moment because everything is on mute. I feel like he's here but not in the way I want him to be.

I've heard all the clichés about how the teacher is quiet during the test, but it stinks. My confidence isn't where I thought it would be. Anticipations of judgement have set in. I don't want to fail. I don't know if I even know what failure is. Because the truth is, it's not the failure that haunts me—it's the laughter. It's the confirmation that I'm just as dumb as I've always assumed I was. It's the childhood insecurity being confirmed in the exposure of this assignment. I don't know if I can handle that type of rejection. I don't know if I can endure that type of negative confirmation. I'm destined to fail at things ... it's life. I just don't want it to be this.

My favorite gospel artist, Kirk Franklin, posted something on X/Twitter that hit me. He said that

"Fear is nothing but contaminated faith. It's believing what the enemy says. FAITH is believing what God says.[1]"

Now first off GOAT Franklin, nobody asked you. Secondly, God I see you. I believe Kirk was saying it's contaminated because you still believe in something happening, just not what God said. You "believe" in an outcome, just not a positive one.

Fear puts its hope in pessimism, while faith puts its hope in God. Fear is the brick wall that has my motivation at bay. It's not that I don't want to write this book ... it's that I don't want to fail at this book. I don't want to be laughed at. I don't want the embarrassment. But more than that, I don't want to be disobedient, so I just keep writing. I don't even know if this entry will help anyone. But it is me in real time, having a real dilemma with finishing. I was unhappy not seeing this type of transparency amongst those who were supposed to inspire us. I guess God said, "How about you do it." Meh.

Yeah that's it. I'll see you next chapter. I just realized I didn't even put a "Food for Thought" in this one. It is what it is.

CHAPTER TWENTY-THREE
Book Cover

I'm not easily annoyed but there are a few things that bother me on the spot. One of those is wasting my time on purpose. I'm trying to work on that. As a matter of fact, let me give you an example. You'll be proud.

Late last night I had a whole ordeal of issues. As I told you before, I'm a part of The Omega Psi Phi Fraternity Incorporated. My chapter is The Mighty Persevering Alpha Delta Mu Chapter at the University of North Florida. For those who aren't familiar with the "Divine Nine," you may be a little lost right now. But we are the best organization out of nine historically black fraternities and sororities. I just lost a few smiles for those who are in the eight others, but we know it's all love. Smile, Greek. Let's have fun. Anyway my chapter just had their probate show to introduce our new initiates to the campus. It was a great show. As it's said in my frat "it was OWT!" It was extremely cold but nonetheless OWT! For those unfamiliar with the word "owt" (out) it's an extremely good adjective for any person, place, or thing.

After the show my chapter brothers needed to take the huge grill we borrowed back. The only issue was that it was unable to latch without a truck. So I went to the closest store which was Walmart. However because of how late it was they were closed. Whatever happened to twenty-four hour Walmart? I think the pandemic killed that. Darn you, COVID. But at this point I had to drive to Walgreens. I was in a rush to get back quickly so I could go home. Luckily, I found a lock in the store. I almost ran to the register to purchase it, but when I got there, things were slowed down almost to a halt. I was third in line, so my expectation was to get out of there quickly. But as I stood there almost itching to go, I felt something scratching my patience too long.

Have you ever sat at a light waiting and you wait so long that you start inching up to see if the sensor in the ground caught your car? You don't let the street be completely clear and you start contemplating whether it's worth it to just risk and run it. Yeah it was feeling like that. So as my patience ran thin like long distance runners, I looked up to see what the holdup was.

At the front of the line was an older woman, but by her appearance, it was apparent she was unhoused. However, she pulled out a physical check. When they scanned it through the system, it declined. Unmoved, she pulled her purse up slowly and then searched for a small pocket book that she pulled her cards out of. They, too, were declined but I could tell she knew they would. I couldn't understand what would cause her to do this. Why would you waste all of our time?

Mentally, I lost it when the cashier called for the manager who had already come by once. The cashier asked for a full void of all the items brought to the counter. The lady then walked out of the store, slowly pushing her buggy filled with black bags of her personal possessions. At this point the guy in front of me looked at me with the wide-eyed "what was all that" face. You know it's real when strangers become associates from a shared debacle. I shrugged my shoulders in our connected frustration and then the manager arrived. The cashier immediately said, "I knew she we going to do that, she's done this before."

At this point I'm extra confused and admittedly frustrated. But the manager's response left my jaw on the floor. She said, "Yeah she's done that to me too, but I don't blame her, it's cold out there." I paused, and my last hour flashed before my eyes, but God forced his grace goggles on my face. I drove to Walgreens in a car so heated that I had to turn the temperature down. I was rushing so I could get back to an actual home. I was frustrated with someone who was milking a moment just to get some heat. Yeah I felt like scum. I especially felt ungrateful, realizing how blessed I was.

In that moment I realized the world consisted of people who wished they were in positions I've complained about. I've complained in my warm house, laying on my couch, while sipping tea. I've been blessed in ways I'll never be able to understand. But the travesty comes when my blessing blocks my ability to access my humanity. Some of us are just one paycheck away from being that beautiful soul who needed a moment of warmth.

God, forgive me for forgetting not just how far I've come, but for the favor that protected me from things I've never endured.

CHAPTER TWENTY-FOUR
Ready Ain't Waiting for You

What if God has a directive in the dark? What if there is an assignment in the night before the joy comes in the morning? How do you handle not knowing everything you would like to know but still being faithful to what he commands?

Now for my lady readers, I hope you don't take this next example to heart but I think you will understand. Ladies who like to put on all the trimmings before going out are usually late. Now before you say I'm wrong, ask yourself if it's true. If it isn't, think of your girlfriend who likes to dress up every time she goes anywhere. Is she usually the late one? But I believe to a certain point ladies like to, as they say, make sure their face is "beat" before they leave the house. Hopefully by the time you read this, that last phrase isn't old.

My wife is notorious for getting ready before we go out anywhere. She acts like I gave her PTSD because, as she explains it, I like to kidnap her. I will tell her we are going one place, then end up going to a few places. Back then she would say I'm not dressed to go anywhere other than the place you said we were going. Now she won't get in the car with me unless she has dressed for any place we may end up. I think it's an overreaction, but then I realized I add stops when we leave so it makes sense.

What if God is calling you to an assignment and you look at yourself in the mirror and think no matter how much makeup and foundation you put on you are still not ready? What if God says I need you "as is" because to him how you look now is perfect. What do you do when God says you are ready when you don't feel like you look ready? How do you deal with the uncomfortability of feeling like you are not ready and God disagrees? In this argument, who's correct? Psst ... come here and let me let you in on a little secret—it's not you.

There was a man by the name of Gideon whom God called to save Israel. The beginning of his story is interesting from the jump.

> The angel of the Lord appeared to Gideon. He said, "Mighty warrior, the Lord is with you."
>
> (Judges 6:12)[1]

Now this scripture seems regular until you notice one thing. There is no indication of Gideon ever being in a battle. He's never been in a war. He's never led any army. So why would God refer to him as a warrior with no evidence? I'm glad you asked.

God will call you what you are before you exhibit any of the characteristics of it. Yup, so the visions you see of yourself that are different from who you are now, depict who you will become. That assignment in your spirit, that you keep saying isn't you, actually is.

I remember being a youth pastor and one of my kids walked into church high as a kite. Red eyes were lower than gas prices in the nineties. I could tell that weed was strong. When he walked by I hugged him and started talking to him.

I'm not going to lie. My initial reason was probably to mess with him and watch him do his best not to act like he was high. Everybody knows it's hard. I remember being so high one time that I was walking down a hall and the walls seemed to keep extending as I walked, but that's a story for another day. We listen and we don't judge.

Anyway, while we were talking, I said to him, "You're a preacher, aren't you." To this day there are two instances I've seen someone sober up quick, and this was definitely one of them. He looked at me with a focus that previously seemed unattainable for him. He said, "I be having dreams about being in the pulpit." He and I were both in shock. That one instance changed him.

He eventually became more vocal in services and a youth leader for a short time. I called him what I saw in the spirit, not what he was at the time. He was living in tomorrow's testimony, but I wasn't waiting for tomorrow to tell him what he was going to be.

Maybe God is doing the same for you. You are not what you will be but God ain't waiting for your first battle to call you mighty warrior—not because of where you are but because of what you are. Simply said, your environment can be bad but that doesn't make you bad. You can even know you are involved in something outside of your calling and God will still say your assignment is your assignment. You are who you are. Some of us need to know we haven't sinned our way out of God's calling.

> Philip found Nathanael and told him, "We have found the one whom Moses wrote about in the Law. The prophets also wrote about him. He is Jesus of Nazareth, the son of Joseph." "Nazareth! Can anything good come from there?" Nathanael asked. "Come and see," said Philip.
>
> (John 1:45-46)[2]

One day someone may ask can anything good come from your city. They may ask can anything good come from your neighborhood. They may even ask can anything good come from your family. You will be the proof that it can. As bad as Nazareth was it still produced the greatest man to ever exist.

You are not so big of a mess that God can't work through you. You have not done so much that God can't use you. Now you will have people who may tell you otherwise, but what is man's word to God's Word?

The Word says once we repent that our sins in God's eyes are as far as the east is from the west, meaning he's not even thinking about them anymore. But our guilt is the reason we hold up our forward movement.

American Christian author and speaker, Joyce Meyers, once said[3] that guilt is our way of trying to pay for what Jesus has already paid for. She goes on to explain how it's because it seems wrong to us—that we do wrong and God forgives us instantly. In short, we punish ourselves according to what makes sense as a right punishment for our crimes. I get it. It's really hard to believe how merciful God is.

There is a scripture that says God is not a man that he should lie. I know that the scripture in its entirety means one thing but the beginning always blesses me. God is not a man, meaning the things that we would do cannot be compared to him.

We often put our characteristics on God. But he is not a man so when he says he has forgiven us, he means it. You are brand new in his eyes. The struggle is admitting that we haven't forgiven ourselves.

One thing I have learned to do is accept "today's me," and "yesterday's me" are two different people. I've seen so many people look back in embarrassment without any grace for what they didn't know. Sure you know now, not to give your heart to the wrong person. But it took that heartbreak to teach you. Stop judging the "pre-lesson" you. If you didn't go through that and learn it, you would still be making the same mistakes. They say, "Hindsight is 20/20."

Don't allow the retrospective thoughts to torment your current place of maturation. You were young, inexperienced, and yes, you were a little hardheaded. Some of us may even be saying I wasn't that young. Me neither. I've got current bad choices I've been mad that I've made. But at the end of the day repent, receive the forgiveness, and move on.

In the 2016 movie *Sully*, Tom Hanks brilliantly plays the role of Chelsey "Sully" Sullenberger. Sully is known for being the hero pilot that saved his 155 passengers after engine failure, by landing in the Hudson River. The movie shows how he and his copilot were scrutinized for the landing and questioned as to whether he could have landed in a better area. There were even simulations showing how pilots had successfully landed the plane. However it was later discovered that the pilots had had hours of practice runs to perfect their ability to land the plane. This of course was unfair because it left no room for split second decisions and human error. The simulation was immediately changed to account for human error, and all attempts from that point on were fails. This left them as heroes.

Our issue is that we are often doing practice runs after the fact of what we could have done, rather than making room for human error. You made decisions with no trial and error. You were in the thick of it. Forgive yourself and live in your purpose. If God forgave you, who are you not to forgive you? You aren't greater than him. So if he's good with it, you be good with it.

What if your purpose has a purpose for you? What if within your purpose you will begin to exhibit the characteristics you wish you could now? Purpose has an exchange. At the same time you are contributing to change, you are also being changed. That person you see in your dreams of who God wants you to be is on the other side of you doing what he told you to do.

At the end of every sermon I would always use this same example for the invitation to salvation. I often hear of people saying they need to get their life together before they make the decision to come to Christ, but that's not how it works. It's like trying to take a bath without using soap or water. No one washes off before they get into the shower. They just get in. That's how you are called to come to Christ.

"Come to me, all you who are tired and are carrying heavy loads. I will give you rest."
(Matthew 11:28)[4]

It's not after you get it together, rather it's after you let Jesus in that you begin to clean up your life. It's him that gives you rest.

You can read all the self-help books and go to all the seminars you want. They will only be a Band-Aid on a huge wound. It's in him that your life begins to change, not before him. What if your purpose matches your salvation? What if you need to first begin to volunteer at the church while you are living in a sinful lifestyle and see the volunteering change your heart?

This may make the Saints clutch their pearls but the problem is the church typically wants you to leave the streets before you can move in the church. In reality it could be your involvement in the church that helps you stop. God tells you to walk away from that to get to this.

There may be a double life situation to start it off. If you are super deep you might want to go to the next paragraph because this may mess with your Jesus a little. But some of your life may be a pulling stage. You have not exited but are in the exit. Slight transparency moment—there are more people in the church living a double life than you think. But there is a grace for changing.

Now don't get me wrong— there is no room for accepting your life of sin, as that mindset comes with no plans to change. We are not in the church to breed lukewarm Christians. However, we are here removing the thought of perfection. You won't even be perfect when you finally feel like you've gotten yourself together. Come as you are expecting to evolve from how you came. Notice the issues and allow God in to make the changes necessary for improvements in your life. Just don't get discouraged with the inevitable failures that come as you are changing.

Marble sculptures are never finished on day one. Matter of fact they look more like a block of marble on the first day than they do a sculpture. But gradually that image changes with the days. If you end up sleeping with that person again, repent and thank God for progress. All it took back in the day was a late night text and you were on your way. But now it took a week. Eventually that week becomes a month. Then that month becomes a few months. Then that becomes a year until it becomes nothing at all.

We are addicted to the theory that all change should be immediate, and addictions should stop cold turkey. Trust me ... God can drastically reduce your desires to nothing. But if that isn't your testimony know that the process is still acceptable to God.

Now I know there are those who may not agree but I'll say it louder before I retract my statements. There are people out there who need to know God still loves them while they are struggling, not after they get it under control. His love is unconditional for a reason. He's not just calling you to help his people, he's also calling you to save YOUR life. God loves to use impossible heroes to change impossible situations. He loves to use the least of us to impact the most of us.

In response to the angel telling him his purpose Gideon said this…

"Pardon me, sir," Gideon replied, "but how can I possibly save Israel? My family group is the weakest in the tribe of Manasseh. And I'm the least important member of my family."

(Judges 6:15)[5]

God has a thing for using the least to do the most. You are not let off the hook because you are the black sheep of your family. It might be the qualifier. David, the great slayer of Goliath, was the youngest of seven brothers. He was so low in his family's eyes that when the prophet came to anoint the next king his father, Jesse, brought out all his brothers and not him. Jesse didn't even consider that the next king would be David. Who told Gideon that he was the least? It may have been his family. God's ranking and man's ranking often clash.

You might be looking at the fact that you never listen, and God is interested in your ability to stand on your own when others disagree. You may be known for being a fighter, and God plans to use that spirit to fight for the kingdom. Whatever your issue God has found a silver lining he plans to use. There's more to you then your issues, and God intends to show you in serving him.

Many times knuckleheads are misdirected leaders. When I worked at an after-school program years ago there was a young man known to be a trouble maker. He was so bad everybody believed there was no changing him. He could care less about rules or authority. In the course of his life someone introduced him to music, and he picked up the horn. Instantly his life changed. He became a great student overnight and an exceptional musician. It settled him.

What if your purpose becomes your horn? It could be the music that settles you down and allows for a focus that few saw in you. But you won't learn it until you pick it up. Moses murdered a man in his youth. David sent a man to war solely to kill him. Peter denied Jesus three times. Adam and Eve caused the great fall from God's presence. Jacob was a trickster. Yet all of them eventually became what God wanted them to be. So what's your excuse? You are exactly who you are meant to be to do exactly what God has preordained you to do.

Contrary to popular belief, God knew every sin you would do well before you were born and still decided he wanted you to be born. So pick your head up and let's get moving. You've got this, and if you don't, God does. You are not so big of a mess that God can't use you.

God spoke all of creation into existence. He is the reason the earth can spin on an axis that sits in the universe perched on nothing at all. He parted the sea for Moses. He caused fire to come down from the heavens for Elijah. He gave Samson the power to kill a small army with the jawbone of a donkey. He paused the sun in the middle of a battle for his people to win. If he did these great things for others, why would he stop exercising his power because our issues seem insurmountable? Simply put, he wouldn't. We are not a paradox that is unfixable for God. We are not so complicated of a problem that God has no solution.

Trust me, he's got this. As we learned in a previous chapter, we are not so terrible that God can't use us. My greatest example to live by is knowing that Moses had a speech impediment. However, according to Acts 7:22, NIRV[6], "Moses was taught all the knowledge of the people of Egypt. He became a powerful speaker and a man of action." Now how could he have a speech impediment, yet later be known as "powerful in speech"? You will be surprised at how much you can accomplish on the other side of trusting God in spite of your issue.

Never wait for the vision God has for you to make sense to you. Faith is the substance of things unseen. So if you can't see it, that actually makes sense.

At first Moses basically said, "God I don't get this, why me? I know there is somebody else that can do this." God was so upset by this "soft no" that he planned to kill Moses. If it weren't for Zipporah, his wife, stepping in, someone else may have parted the Red Sea. It seems harsh because Moses appears to have been humble. Most of us would quietly applaud this. But it brings up a harsh reality. You can fool all of us, but you can't fool God.

To understand this, we have to address humility. It is the obedience to serve God however and wherever he desires. This is the truth of humility before the Lord. So any other action that goes against his will is not humility. This is also why you cringe as you watch people mess up on the stage that God called you to. I've learned that places of your agitation are often your calling. God does not respect a soft no. Don't let the masses fool you, if he wants you somewhere you don't want to go. You can't negotiate with kind words.

CHAPTER TWENTY-FIVE
Fear vs Ready

I've known my pastor, Bishop Hill, for a while. We were in a theatrical play together more than a decade ago. Many of those who were in the play now go to The Citadel Church as well.

When we met I didn't even know he was a pastor because he was so down to earth. He also was one of those guys who didn't feel the need to tell people he was a pastor. That's what I loved about him as a person. I'd been eyeing the ministry for years and had already told my wife that if we ever left our past church we would be going to his church. She emphatically agreed. Well the day came and little did I know what was to happen next.

When we joined, he took me and my wife to dinner with his wife, Lady Kim, and it was a surreal experience to say the least. The experience made me wish we had joined years before. But there was one thing he said under his breath as we left them. I can hear it like it was yesterday. He said, "Ok, I don't let my elders sit." In other words I won't be waiting a long time to put you up to teach.

Of course I thought he was just talking. There was no way this man was going to let me, a newcomer, teach at his church. People don't do that. Fast forward (but not too fast) two weeks after that conversation —we were finishing up our midweek Bible study and I got a tap on the shoulder by a guy I had never met. "Pastor told me to tell you that you are teaching next Tuesday." Wait, what?!

First off who is this random guy telling me what Bishop said (side note: I later got to know him at a church function and he's a really cool dude)? Secondly ...WHAT?! I immediately looked over in Bishop's direction only to see him looking at me pointing while talking to my wife. That's when I knew it was true. Immediately my nerves were shot, and I couldn't believe he was actually serious about putting me up. The traitor, also known as my wife, walked up with a smirk on her face and said, "Did you get the message?" Yeah, I got it, but why didn't you tell him I wasn't ready?

Food for Thought:
Sometimes your spouse sees you on the level you don't believe you are ready for. It's not their job to make you comfortable all the time. Sometimes that necessary push comes from home.

And that sounds real deep and spiritual but I wasn't trying to hear any of that at the moment. The next day I texted Bishop to confirm because, in his usual jovial nature, he walked away before I could contest it in person. Here's the text.

Me:
I'm just here to verify that you want me to teach next week lol
Also do you have a topic that you desire for me to teach?
Also watching me react from afar is diabolical lol

Bishop:
Verification complete! Yes indeed sir, we need the Word and you've got it for us next week. No specific topic.
Prepare for 30 min time frame
I am hollering!! LOL That head wipe was intense!!

Me:
I was like first off who is this dude telling me what the Bishop is

saying,

    look at the devil trying to attack me after a good Word. LOL
Then I looked over and saw ur face and knew LOL

As we texted, a God download entered my mind. All I heard God say was, "Ready ain't waiting for you." I knew then that not only was this the lesson, but it was also a testimony for the night. So I began to research and gather stories that helped me to write the lesson.

The most impactful story was told by one of my favorite evangelists, Cliffe Knechtle. It's a true story about a married couple named Mark and Susan. Mark was a dedicated military man. Unfortunately, Susan suddenly began to lose her eyesight and became fully blind. This left her in a depressive state. But Mark began to comfort her and told her that they would work together to help her get her life back.

Every day they worked on normalizing her life as much as possible. He took her to work and helped her learn how to do her job blind. After a while he let her know he couldn't keep this up for much longer because he was constantly showing up to work late. She freaked out immediately. But he assured her that he would help her to the bus stops, help her cross the streets, and walk her to the job to create a habitual routine.

They practiced this up until the day came that he could no longer assist. She went through the routine the exact same way they had practiced. Every day for a week she executed every marker with precision. She made it to Friday, and the bus driver said, "Ma'am you are one lucky lady." She responded by saying, "Stop it, I am a blind woman." Then the bus driver responded by saying, "Yes this is true, but all week a man in a military uniform has been waiting at your stop. He never takes his eyes off of you. When you cross the street he's watching you. When you go up the stairs he's watching you. As soon as you close the door he stands tall, salutes you, and blows you a kiss. Then he walks away."

She knew then it was her husband. She'd been feeling alone in a world on her own, and had no clue that her husband had been there the whole time. In Ephesians 5 we learn that Christ is referred to as the Bridegroom and the church is his bride. This is what makes this story so beautiful. He has no intention of leaving us out there. However, sometimes what seems to be a separation is simply an effort to show us that we can do the very things we dread.

Food for Thought:
Some uncomfortable pushes are necessary for us to reach the heights God intends for us to attain.

Baby birds would never learn to fly if they weren't first pushed out from the comfort of the nest. It's instinct that kicks in when they hit the air, and what they didn't know they were capable of becomes second nature.

What if you are a savant at a skill that you will never know because you refused to try? I spoke about instinct earlier. I believe we all have a spiritual instinct that kicks in as soon as we hit the air. But the fear of the cliff has us locked out of rooms, while holding the keys in our hand.

If you are going to leave the nest, you will have to fall. But the truth is we don't fear the air. Instead, we fear the ground. You can't achieve the goal without facing the possibility of the ground. We would rather have a detailed layout of how this is going to work out. However, God only shows us those in the past that he's helped fly. The Bible is full of success stories. But what do you do when God taps you on the shoulder and says, "I want you to be my next story"? What happens when he removes your crutch and says, "No, lean on me now, not your own understanding"?

There is a Native American story about the Cherokee tribe. It is believed that back in the day there was a particular rite of passage for boys to become men. Late at night their father would lead them to a stump in the middle of the forest. Fathers then would blindfold their sons and leave. The boy was expected to sit at the stump alone through the night until the break of day. "Nope, not I," says Dez Demps. My nerves would be shot.

Can you imagine the nerves going through the poor kid's body? It's funny how much you can hear when your sight is removed. I know he could hear the wolves in the background and everything rustling in the bushes. He could hear the crickets and frogs. He probably felt the wind against his sweating forehead. Let's put the kickstand down for a creepy moment. Have you ever felt something crawling on you and quickly hit yourself only to realize it was just your mind playing tricks on you? I know he had a few moments of feeling things crawling on him. But he had to stay still to prove he could endure that night as a man.

Standing still and trusting God can be hard when busy work is a good distraction from fear. Some of us would rather swing blindfolded like a crazy person in case something runs up. But what we don't realize is we are tiring ourselves out before something actually happens that needs that energy.

The hard part can be sitting still and letting God do his part without tinkering. It's like that sibling who asked for help to tie their shoe but keeps grabbing the strings, thinking they're helping. God may be saying, "Move out of the way and let me do it."

Back to our Cherokee warrior ... I know he can hear all kinds of animals that could possibly devour him in the distance. He's probably even imagined some of the noises in his head. It amazes me how many things the mind can mix in with actual reality, especially when danger lurks around us. It feels encompassing like an eerie fog. Paranoia has made many of us make mistakes in fear of possible outcomes rather than actual ones.

NFL quarterbacks are judged by this very thing ... not their height, speed, or even talent. But poise is judged by how well they stand under pressure, while surrounded by men often twice their size, who desire to sack them.

In the same way, the young Cherokee warrior is challenged in his area of poise. He's also challenged to not listen to understandable paranoia. He sits on the stump but he's really sitting in the darkness of his own thoughts. He listens to animal steps in the grass and fights the paranoia that says remove the blindfold and run. It's the battle of wits.

I imagine that once he sees the brightening of the sunrise from the inside of the blindfold, he removes it quickly. His heart is probably beating out of his chest. But what he sees astonishes him. His father was sitting on the stump the whole time, protecting him from possible danger. He had felt alone for a whole night but the joy in the morning was met with knowing his father had been there the whole time.

Food for Thought:
      Feeling alone and being alone are two totally different things. This life will come with the "feeling" of being alone. But you will never experience the actuality of "being" alone. God is ever present and never leaves your side, no matter how dark the day is. It's true—sometimes he is silent. But he will never abandon you.

Isn't that the craziest part of life that we don't talk about enough? Although the boy couldn't see, he was still seen. What I've learned is that we are so focused on being able to see what's next, that we can't see what's now. We can't notice amongst all the noises the sound of our Father sitting right next to us.

Life's noise is so distracting we don't even notice God being right there. If we can't see him, he must not be there. We don't realize our eyes aren't the most important in our faith seasons.

Whether you want to accept it or not there are some ordained dark seasons sent from God. Just like the boy had to stand still, he sometimes wants you to stand still and know he is God. The only way to know he is God is to stay where he told you to when you feel the necessity to move. You can't know God is a keeper unless you suffer a season where you need to be kept.

Just know that if you are in a season where God is quiet, the silence doesn't remove the protection. The silence also doesn't mean you don't need to talk. You can talk even if you don't get a response. You don't need a response to know he is listening. He's on the stump with you. He's standing at the bus stop as you get off. He's saluting you as you do a good job of sticking to the routine of what you practiced in blind praise. You know what to do. Maintain your worship in the dark.

"Even though I walk through the darkest valley, I will not be afraid. You are with me. Your shepherd's rod and staff comfort me."

(Psalm 23:4)[1]

Like many others I love this scripture. However, it never says anything about God talking. But he's never needed to talk to be with you. Just know that if you are in a season where God is quiet, the silence doesn't remove the protection.

CHAPTER TWENTY-SIX
Just Another Tuesday

In college, I taught a Bible study called YVOG. We met every Tuesday at nine o'clock in the evening. As the years continued I noticed a pattern. Every Tuesday was a struggle for me, like clockwork. Crazy, unexpected, and frustrating things happened every Tuesday. I would write messages on my Facebook feed, and it would suddenly delete and I'd have to start over. I would send inspirational emails out to everyone, and they would delete out of nowhere just before I hit send. Random frustrations would happen on the job. There was always some unexpected monkey wrench to derail the day.

It happened so much that I found myself saying the same thing every week, "it's just another Tuesday." I knew what it was but it didn't stop it from bothering me each week. I was fulfilling my assignment for the Lord, while simultaneously causing an issue for the devil. Tuesday was the pinnacle of the attack because of the Bible study. If it was really a bad Tuesday, I knew Bible study was going to be good. I just got used to it. It's something I live by to this day. I don't sweat it anymore.

Now it's not that I don't get disappointed, I just don't get swayed by disappointment. If the long message deletes, I take a breather, then I start writing again. Without fail the second try is always better than the initial one. I knew I was in a fight. But what the devil didn't realize is that as long as I was in a fight, I knew the devil saw me as a threat.

That's exactly what I wanted to be. Spiritual warfare is a fight, and I became accustomed to his jabs and hooks. But I don't ever think he got used to my determination uppercut.

Food for Thought:
You can't be in a fight and not expect the opponent to fight back. It's easier to fight when you realize you are in one. Just understand that there are no haymakers that can take you out.

"But no weapon used against you will succeed."
(Isaiah 54:17a)[1]

This scripture is literally the hill that Christians think makes them super Saiyan. No, Goku, it just lets you know you won't be defeated. It doesn't mean you won't get hit. So you can stop yelling in your living room … KAMEHAMEHA! That's a Dragon Ball reference for those wondering. Just because you win doesn't mean you go uninjured. The issue is we stop not because we lost. We stop because we didn't expect to be hit that hard. You didn't expect God to want you to continue with a black eye. Not giving up takes grit to recognize that going down is not an option.

Beethoven wrote some of the most beautiful music the world has ever heard. After a while he began to go deaf. Can you imagine how devastating it would've been to be a composer who couldn't hear? It's a good excuse to not compose ever again. No one would judge him for not writing music. I mean how could you continue without being able to hear what you wrote? But he could still hear. He had composed for so long the notes were committed to memory. When completely deaf, he composed one of his greatest pieces known as "The Ninth." He went on to create more music despite his disadvantage.

In her youth Harriet Tubman was once hit on the head with a huge rock by a white man. It caused her to have narcolepsy. She would randomly fall asleep, which they then called "spelling spells." Can you imagine how that could affect her while leading slaves on the Underground Railroad? Think of how much of a safety issue that would be. The possibility of getting caught while running at night could be enough reason to give up fighting for her cause. But the dilemma was not enough to stop her. She trusted God so much that she didn't let an understandable problem stop her. This is why she's my favorite hero. Harriet treated brick walls like hurdles. Maybe it's time for us to do the same.

Food for Thought:
       Sometimes difficulty is the prerequisite to importance. Whatever the devil attacks he fears.

I'm a nineties kid so *Teenage Mutant Ninja Turtles* are unmatched when it comes to cartoons. I think the pizza industry owes those four turtles everything. But if you know the story, their development came from a broken test tube in the sewer. Four regular turtles walked in this green goo, and it changed them into fighting machines. They went from being slow, harmless turtles to skilled ninjas that struck fear in Shredder and the foot clan.

At times if you feel attacked, you are proving the goo you were made in. God is the goo that made you a threat. You were fearfully and wonderfully made. You've activated the devil's fight or flight reflexes. And now that the devil feels backed in a corner where he can't escape the anointing God placed on you, he's fighting back. His last hope is to derail you with the distraction of disappointment. Don't ever step off the track simply because the unexpected happened.

Motivational Speaker Simon Sinek Johnson once said, "There is no such thing as a plan that goes according to plan.[2]" But Romans 8:28[3] says "We know that in all things God works for the good of those who love him. He appointed them to be saved in keeping with his purpose."

Even a bad result in your eyes is still a good result in God's eyes.

Accept there are factors in your plan that God had not yet made you aware of. It may have a few twists and turns you didn't expect. But nothing is outside of his range to work it together for your good.

We often forget we are finite creatures. We have limitations. We can't correctly predict the future but God is the same today, yesterday, and forevermore. He's in all time so he knows the outcome. His plan is to prosper us. It is never too harm us. So even when the going gets tough, remember, the tough gets going. That's an old saying but it fits.

This little monkey wrench isn't enough to derail you. It's enough to frustrate you. It's enough to make you angry. It's enough to make you want to scream although it's never enough to make you quit, because quitting is never an option. But screaming is ok.

Now one sentence that may have confused you is the "he's in all time," part. Let me explain. This is important because prayer is necessary in times like these. But I don't see a lot of people explaining what it can do. I need you to grab a pen or pencil. Now grab the middle of it. We all have seen how toddlers use crayons. Before they learned how to correctly write, they grab the whole crayon to color with. That's how you need to be grabbing your pen or pencil.

Now, imagine there are little notches under your fingers on the pen/pencil. Those notches represent years. Imagine your hand is God. Based on the notches, your hand is just as much in the notches in the front of the pen/pencil as it is in the back. The pencil is the timeline. We are all subject to the notches.

We can't exist beyond the notches we are in. God, who stands outside of time, is in all time at once. It is not the timeline that has God. It is God that has time. You can't be subject to what you've created. So why is this example important? When you pray, you send messages and requests to a being who is already where you are going. He can respond to your request for tomorrow because he's already in tomorrow's notches. It's not that you pray for him to do it when the day comes. He can do it already before the day gets here.

I know this is a lot to process, but you need to know the reach of your God. He can be setting up your year today because he's already in your tomorrow, right now. He's already in the whole week. He's already in the whole year. Your future is under his command, not the other way around. So pray and anticipate what he can do beyond your limitations.

CHAPTER TWENTY-SEVEN
Unwanted Grace

> "If your brother or sister sins against you, go to them. Tell them what they did wrong. Keep it between the two of you. If they listen to you, you have won them back. But what if they won't listen to you? Then take one or two others with you. Scripture says, 'Every matter must be proved by the words of two or three witnesses.' But what if they also refuse to listen to the witnesses? Then tell it to the church. And what if they refuse to listen even to the church? Then don't treat them as a brother or sister. Treat them as you would treat an ungodly person or a tax collector."
>
> (Matthew 18:15-17)[1]

I've read this scripture many times and have interpreted things I believe have helped me to mend broken heart trauma of my past. But one thing that has offended me was the effort of the offended. We live by an unspoken expectation that is not biblical even though it would be convenient.

We say that if you wrong me, it is your job to correct the offense, not mine. We will even go as far as to say that if you never correct the issue, then the relationship obviously wasn't that important to you in the first place. I believe we have had many broken friendships, relationships, and family dynamics ripped apart from this type of ineffective thinking. We often champion conflict resolution for others until the resolving comes to our doorstep. It would seem that the most comfortable thing to do is to throw the baby out with the bath water. We would rather lose the connection entirely rather than address the issue. I've been there and have lost a lot of time with allies I characterized as enemies simply because I didn't want to be the one that initiated the reconciliation. I mean why does it have to be me? Why am I expected to do such?

We often say we desire to be close to the character of God until his character disturbs our logical frustration. Matthew 18 shows the proper protocol for conflict resolution. We may not agree with it. We may not even like it, but if it is to be conducted correctly, this is the course of action.

I remember having a very heated conversation with one of my closest friends. He wondered why I had been so distant for years. He noticed I had been stand offish and wanted to know the issue. It was a hard conversation because I wasn't budging. I was deeply hurt and pissed to say the least. When we cycled through the conversation, I finally told him there was a lie told about me, and I was angry he never defended me.

We ran in the same tight-knit circles, and I was convinced he hadn't had my back. The crazy part is that once I said the lie, he responded in a way that only showed shock. He hadn't even heard it until then. I instantly realized how much time I had lost from a friend, caused by a simple misunderstanding.

I had been convinced of an unproven thing. The point of reaching out to your offender is for the initial clarity. Your brother or sister may be unaware of the offense. As I've begrudgingly said before, I'm a diehard Jacksonville Jaguars fan. If you are a real fan you will never forget two things. The first one is that Myles Jack wasn't down in the game against the Patriots in the 2017 AFC Championship. The second is the 1999 season where the Jags went 15-0 against the whole league, but 0-3 against the Titans.

There is a deep disgust for the Titans amongst Jaguar fans. We could be having a great year and they, the opposite, and for some reason, they would end up beating us. But I told my wife something that hurts me to this day. With the stats, games, and mishaps, I'm convinced the Titans are totally unaware of this rivalry. I mean think about it. Your team always seems to do well against us. You often win. You've watched your team have great success there. So why would you be mad? If anything, you would look forward to the meeting.

We as an organization have not provided a real reason for Tennessee to feel the disgust we have. But clearly, we have an issue that isn't reciprocated. I've even seen multiple pictures on social media where Jaguars fans visit Nashville for random reasons and make sure they go by the stadium to take a picture of them flicking a certain finger at the team's facilities. But I've never seen a Titans' fan do the same.

I know it sounds crazy but what if you have a rivalry that only exists in your mind? What if, by some chance, you are the only one as they say in the South, "feuding" with someone? This will never be discovered unless you reach out.

Now let's be honest. This isn't always the case. There are times when the person knows what they did and yet they still have refused to reach out. Let's take it back to the garden. If you read in Genesis 3 you are made aware of the fall of Man. God tells Adam he can have all the Garden of Eden offers but he can't have the fruit from one tree.

Imagine this ... you gave someone actual life. You gave them a place to stay. You gave them food to eat. You gave them a job. You even hooked them up with a spouse. You are the reason they have everything they have. All you asked was for them to leave one thing alone. Now let's be clear—you gave them all of these things without them doing anything to earn said spoiling. They don't even have the capacity to give you back an equal amount of gratitude for the blessings and favor. But at the whisper of another being (Satan) who had also done you wrong, they listened to him instead of obeying you and did what you asked them not to do. That is the ultimate betrayal.

People often discuss it being too harsh of God to punish man the way he did without first addressing everything. However, the Bible is clear—the wages of sin is death. We deserved death for our disobedience, but lovingly he still clothed us and kept us alive.

Think of how betrayed you have been when you have given someone more than God gave you and they mistreated the relationship. I know this seems like a farfetched tangent but consider that God never asks us to do what he hasn't provided in an example from his own actions. We broke the relationship and he reached out. We caused the rip that fractured our covenant with God. He then responded by reaching back out to us in Jesus to correct the wrong.

He reached out and made the effort in other instances, too. God reached out by getting Moses's attention in the burning bush. He came to Gideon to deliver his people. He reached out to Mary to tell her she would be the mother of our Savior. For centuries God has been the one reaching out to us despite our continued offenses. He has constantly shown the example of what forgiveness and reconciliation should look like. Apart from abuse and toxicity we have to take our example from God. He's constantly reached out to us prior to the birth of Jesus. He has extended his hand of fellowship in spite of our lack of effort.

We have to accept that our assumption of fairness is a fool's fantasy. We have made it a cultural standard for us to hold grudges until our offender decides to correct the offense, not us. When Jesus went to pray at Gethsemane he only allowed for three disciples to stay close as he prayed. One of them was Peter. It is well documented how close Jesus and Peter were. But in the night of Jesus being arrested he knew his closest friend would deny knowing him.

> Jesus said to him (Peter), "It will happen tonight. Before the rooster crows, you will say three times that you don't know me."
> (Matthew 26:34)[2]

Peter responded to the above scripture, saying he would never do such a thing. But that very night Peter watched as they arrested Jesus and dragged him down the road to see the Sanhedrin. Along the way he was questioned three times if he knew Jesus by those watching the spectacle. He denied his friendship so adamantly that he cursed on the last denial. At that moment of his final denial he heard the crow of a rooster and looked though the crowd to see the eyes of Jesus staring directly at him. It's a chilling thought to think of that moment. Peter, remembering what Jesus had said, ran away weeping because of what he had done.

I always thought this prophetic moment with Jesus was interesting. Why would you say this to Peter prior to the night? There are a few interpretations of course. But lend me your ear for a second. Does Peter's denial revoke all the previous moments of brotherly love between the two? Does his denial become proof of them never truly being friends? I don't believe so. I believe it is a true case of self-preservation outweighing loyalty.

Peter had a human moment that was at the cost of his commitment. It's believed that Peter was in fear of suffering the same fate as Jesus if he was recognized as being associated with him. In his human moment he, in short, disowned his friend.

It always interests me how people often want to be accepted for their human moments but don't want to accept people for their human moments. We've all had bad days that caused us to have attitudes that were less than appealing. But we have little to no room for others to do the same. We want our circumstances to be included in the interpretation of our actions, but we do not want to do that for someone else.

What do you do when someone has acted out of character toward you and they have offended you like they've never done before? I'll tell you how. Follow what Jesus did.

After Jesus was raised from the dead he made some visits. One of those visits was to Peter. Peter had gone fishing. What makes this so significant is that this is what he was doing when Jesus first recruited him to be a disciple. Now this is going to hit differently because forgiveness doesn't always affect you. It can affect the one you forgive.

You'd be surprised at how many vices people go back to simply because they don't feel like they are worthy of forgiveness. Jesus told Peter previously that he would be a fisher of men. However, in Peter's self-disappointment, he reduced himself to the place Jesus found him. Sometimes you must go to the person because they don't feel worthy enough to come to you. What if the reason they haven't reached out is because they are too ashamed to face you? They get why you don't forgive them because they don't either.

Food for Thought:
>
> There are more stories to the narrative of your offense. You may be the only one offended, but you aren't always the only one bound.

When Jesus reconciled with Peter, it ignited a fire with Peter that caused him to be one of the most prolific leaders of Christ. He even was later crucified upside down because he was so devoted to Jesus that he felt unworthy to die the same way.

Reconciled friendships are often much stronger than they were prior to the infraction. My uncle was involved in a major motorcycle accident many years ago. He suffered a few broken bones. But I'll never forget what he told me after he had healed. His broken bones had healed in a way that it would be much harder to break again in the same place. The healing process fortified the bone to make it more durable than before. What was broken between you and your friend can be fortified in a way that it can never be broken again.

I watched a movie by the name of *Cloudy with a Chance of Meatballs 2*. It's a hilarious movie but there were two supposed Chinese proverbs spoken to Flint, the main character. First the sly words of the villain, Chester V, "Stew from a bully is poisoned broth." However, later on his trusted love interest, responded to this phrase by saying, "A bully turned friend will be friend to the end." It reminds me of the cartoons where a character is tempted to make a decision that's either good or evil. Two entities pop up on the character's shoulders—one dressed as an angel, while the other is dressed as a devil. They then talk to plead their case for their preferred action to take. We have a choice no matter what.

The issue we often face is that the right choice is often the harder choice. Right does not always come in a way that feels right. As a matter of fact we can be honest ... some of the most righteous acts of our lives won't even seem fair. But is fair the barrier holding you back from doing the right thing? Are you stuck at fair when God is calling you to make amends? Are you waiting for it to seem right before acting? I'm here to tell you ... you may be waiting in vain.

We often wait for a right rather than causing it to be right. Imagine you and a friend built a bridge out of wood. It took you two years to build it. One day you see the bridge burning, and at the end of the bridge you see your friend holding a torch. If you had access to a hose, are you waiting for them to put down the torch and start spraying? Or are you taking action and spraying to save years of hard work? You may be right ... you didn't cause the fire but if you have the capacity to put it out, it's better to do so than sit by and watch a bridge burn between friends.

We love to say that Christian means Christ-like. Being a Christian is to live a life that emulates the characteristics of God. But as many of us do, we skip over the parts we don't like.

My little brother was notorious for having a healthy appetite when we were kids. He would clean his plate like a grown man. But there was one food he couldn't stand—peas. In our house if you didn't eat your food you had to stay at the table until you finished your plate. I'm sure that is a common rule in the African American culture.

Daniel would clean that plate and stay at the counter for forty-five minutes just looking at the plate. I know that sounds exaggerated but its actually true. He was that stubborn. He even got clever. If you put a napkin next to him he would slide the peas in the napkin and throw them away and act like he ate them. Depending on the day I would even help him out. But if he annoyed me that day I would yell, "Oooh, Ma, Daniel's doing it again." To which he would throw a tantrum and scrunch his little face at me. (Yeah that's right. If you annoyed me, I had no problem being a snitch to get you back as a kid. Don't judge.) But I think grace is something we love to receive but hate to give. We treat grace like a golden banner when we receive it from God and people. But we treat it like Daniel treated those peas when we are asked to give it.

The Lord's Prayer says forgive us as we forgive our debtors. Our forgiveness is contingent upon us forgiving. We have to extend the hand of forgiveness as we receive it. God has extended so much grace to us. It is in his character to do so because he is love. If we are to be Christ-like, then we have to take on his likeness in this opportunity as well.

That's right. I said opportunity. Giving grace to someone is an opportunity to honor God in a way that shows you are his child. It is a clear display of him being your Father. In a previous job, when I went to sports games for high schools, I could see parents in the stands rooting their kids on. Many of them, being former athletes, watched their kids continue the athletic legacy they paved. They saw them displaying the same skills they had at their age. They lived vicariously through the kid in the moment. My favorite moment is when a parent sees their child score. They say "that's my boy," or "that's my girl." They want everyone to know who they got that from.

In pride they need the crowd to know that's my kid because of their action in the game. What if God wants to do the same for you? What if you are on the field of life and God sees you challenging your flesh to initiate the reconciliation? What if he's up there with the angels in the stands cheering you on, and as soon as you score the initial interaction, he yells, "That's my boy/girl."

What a sight to believe in. Jesus knows you don't want to do it. But he did. So as he does so should you. You never know … you may need that bridge later. Don't watch it burn down.

CHAPTER TWENTY-EIGHT
Rags to Riches

When I was a youth pastor I would always tell the kids the same story at the end of service. No one uses a rag to wash off before they take a shower. They just get in. There is no process of pre-cleaning before getting clean. So when it comes to accepting Christ in your life you have to accept the same logic.

I hate there is a narrative out there that we have to be Christ-like before we invite Christ into our lives. God is not requiring you to put down the blunt before you can get saved. He is not requiring you to stop sleeping with that person before you get saved. He is not requiring you to leave that life before you choose life in him. If salvation is a present then why do I have to dress up to receive it? Just give it to me. He desires to give you this gift. You just have to ask for it.

Simply put, salvation is the accepting of Christ as your Savior. He will progress into your Lord over time. You probably will go back to the things you know aren't the best representation of good character after you receive salvation. That will work itself out after a while. But I apologize for the misrepresentation you may have seen. The Word warns Christians not to be so heavenly minded that they are of no earthly good. The church at times is more faithful to a CULTure than they are to the actual faith. So I can understand the frustration.

Take it from me. I'm a reverend, minister, ordained elder, and ordained pastor, and I still feel out of place at times because of not being raised in the church. There is room for you. There is also room for you the way you are.

One of my favorite people to watch on television is former NFL running back, Marshawn Lynch. He has always been himself no matter the environment. He doesn't care what people think he should be like. He is just himself. That's how you should see salvation. God is not trying to change the core of who you are. If you are loud and boisterous, more than likely you will stay that way after salvation. If you love adventure and physical challenges, you will continue to. The only thing that will change is your banner.

Over time you will speak with the Lord, motivating your loud voice. You will have adventures with the Lord on your side. Even if you are a violent person you won't stop being violent as much as you will learn when and how to fight. God needs fighters, too. King David was a fighter. But where you used to fight the people, you will fight for the people. Don't fear the accepting of Christ, and don't walk down that depressing road of unworthiness.

You may be thinking, "Well you don't know what I've done, Dez." Yeah, well you don't know what I've done.

Again, your response may be, "But I'm still struggling with a few things, Dez." Well we have something in common now, don't we? Don't let these words fool you. I was a fool, too. Being honest, I only stopped being a fool because the call to represent him better was higher than my desire to act up. As a matter of fact, let's have a little testimony time. I used to shut a club or party down.

My favorite setting was a house party because there was no room. The more crowded, the better. I loved it when the drinks were flowing, hips were moving, speakers were blasting on a black pole, and a slight hint of weed in the air. The best music had the worst lyrics, and I loved it. I remember as I got older, one of my favorite clubs was Top Flight in Tallahassee, Florida. The Moon was cool from time to time but if I wanted to enjoy myself, I knew Top Flight was the place for me. I always ran to the middle where it was the most convoluted and put in work. One of the hardest things I had to do in life was retire my party animal ways. I love the Lord but I ain't the type to act like I am disgusted by my worldly ways. I'm obedient to my call. But I know who I am.

This seat I take is my sacrifice to represent him well. Not because I'm deep ... be clear ... I have nothing against parties or even dancing. For other people, they may be ok to dance in certain atmospheres. But as for me, I gotta as the people say "sa' down somewhere" when music comes on. It's like a gateway drug for me, a gateway sin if you will.

We all have our gateway situation. You know what you are going to do if you go over there with them. You know if you hang around these friends, what type of stuff you are going to get in. A guy by the name of Joseph in the Bible was tempted by his master's wife. She caught him hanging out in the house by himself while her husband was gone. She wanted him so bad that she grabbed his clothes to get him. But he chose to run out of the house, leaving them in her hand to get away. He knew that if he stayed and played around, he could fall. He went on to be a great man in the kingdom after some years of turmoil. But even this great man of God found himself running from sin.

Whether we are the bishop of a church or a person in the pew, we all have a favorite sin. Nobody is exempt from the particular thing that can make us slip. I went to a conference where host of *Rejoice in the Word* of The Word Network, Bishop George Bloomer, was teaching. The man is a genius and staple of the faith. But he told us about his life and his testimony. He told us of the years he struggled with drug addiction. In a very candid moment, he told us of the struggle of staying sober.

I'll never forget this one thing he said. He used this example that shook me. He looked around in the pulpit and said, "You can fill this stage up with the most beautiful women you can find, and I won't fall. You can put the usual thing that makes the average man fall, and I won't budge. But if you put drugs up here, I'm in trouble." This is coming from one of the most well-respected men in the kingdom you will find. But God still covers him as he continues to do the Lord's will.

When you get saved, Jesus instantly becomes your savior. But you will be at the beginning of him becoming your Lord. The process takes time, and no one is pushing to speed it up. As Bishop Bloomer has even shown in his own example, you may have things you will struggle with for the rest of your life. But one thing you will never have to fear again is the destination of your soul after you die. I know people often talk about hell to non-believers for a scare tactic, but let's identify its truth. God didn't create hell for humans. It was for fallen angels. It's the final judgement meant for Satan and those angels that followed his failed insurrection in heaven.

When we fell from grace by eating the apple, it took us out of alignment with our original destination. It made us align with the judgement of the fallen angels. Salvation simply corrects the broken covenant and realigns us with God's plan for the final destination of our souls after death. Makes sense, doesn't it? See, it's not that deep, but it is that important. If you are reading this and have not accepted Christ in your life, I want you to repeat these following words out loud and accept a gift that keeps on giving.

Say ... Lord Jesus, to you and only you, do I confess that I am a sinner. Through you I repent of my sins. Come into my heart. I make you my Lord, Master, and Savior forever and ever. Amen.

Yup that's right ... it's that simple. If you just received salvation, there are angels in heaven rejoicing at this very moment for you. I pray your life reaches a new height of enjoyment, peace, and fulfillment. I hope you enjoyed the book and until next time. I love you and you can't do anything about it. God bless.

UNACCEPTABLE CHRISTIAN

ABOUT THE AUTHOR

DEZ DEMPS is a seasoned minister with over 22 years of experience in ministry. A former Youth and Young Adult Pastor, he has dedicated his life to guiding and inspiring the next generation. Hailing from Jacksonville, Florida, Dez is also a talented singer and songwriter. His album, *Not Ready*, gained national attention and earned a spot on the charts. Dez is happily married to his wife, Tymerial, and continues to use his voice—both spoken and sung—to impact lives and spread faith.

UNACCEPTABLE CHRISTIAN

Endnotes

Sand Dedication

1. Holy Bible. New International Reader's Version. NIrV Bible. Version 10.16. YouVersion. 2025. App.

Homeland Hate

1. Holy Bible. New International Reader's Version. NIrV Bible. Version 10.16. YouVersion. 2025. App.

100 Random vs 50 Consistent

1. Singh Rathore, Jaspal. "Shocking facts about Bruce Lee." YouTube, uploaded by Learn with Jaspal, 29 Dec., 2023, https://www.youtube.com/shorts/x8fhlVaLcxg.

To Sting or Not to Sting

1. Holy Bible. New International Reader's Version. NIrV Bible. Version 10.16. YouVersion. 2025. App.
2. Holy Bible. New International Reader's Version. NIrV Bible. Version 10.16. YouVersion. 2025. App.

Outta Reach

1. Holy Bible. New International Reader's Version. NIrV Bible. Version 10.16. YouVersion. 2025. App.
2. Holy Bible. New International Revised Version. NIrV Bible. Version 10.16. YouVersion. 2025. App.
3. Holy Bible. King James Version. KJV Bible. Version 10.16. YouVersion. 2025. App.

* * *

Face Value

1. Holy Bible. New International Reader's Version. NIrV Bible. Version 10.16. YouVersion. 2025. App.
2. "Fault Vs Responsibility by Will Smith FULL SPEECH." YouTube, uploaded by WhateverItTakesMotivation, 31 Jan. 2018, https://youtu.be/USsqkd-E9ag?si=5Zmm59HEPWMKAqg7.

Actually Being There

1. Holy Bible. New International Reader's Version. NIrV Bible. Version 10.16. YouVersion. 2025. App.
2. Holy Bible. New International Version. NIV Bible. Version 10.16. YouVersion. 2025. App.

Cinderella Man

1. Holy Bible. New King James Version. NKJV Bible. Version 10.16. YouVersion. 2025. App.
2. Holy Bible. New International Reader's Version. NIrV Bible. Version 10.16. YouVersion. 2025. App.

Wrong Size

1. Holy Bible. New International Revised Version. NIrV Bible. Version 10.16. YouVersion. 2025. App.
2. Holy Bible. New International Revised Version. NIrV Bible. Version 10.16. YouVersion. 2025. App.

Shake 'n Bake

1. First Take. Directed by Brandy Tate, ESPN Enterprises, 2024.
2. Holy Bible. New International Version. NIV Bible. Version 10.16. YouVersion. 2025. App.

Caught in the Bushes

1. T.D. Jakes [@BishopJakes]. "Forgiveness does not exonerate the perpetrator. Forgiveness liberates the victim. It's a gift to give yourself... #DomesticViolenceAwareness." X, 15 Oct. 2017, 8:30 p.m., https://x.com/bishopjakes/status/919722096065998848?s=46. Accessed 8 Jun. 2025.

* * *

Mountain Top

1. The LOX, DMX, and Lil' Kim. "Money, Power & Respect." Money, Power & Respect, Bad Boy Records, 1998. CD.
2. The Notorious B.I.G., Puff Daddy, and Mase. "Mo Money Mo Problems." Life After Death. Bad Boy Records, 1997. CD.
3. Holy Bible. New International Reader's Version. NIrV Bible. Version 10.16. YouVersion. 2025. App.
4. THE MESSAGE: the Bible in Contemporary Language. MSG. Version 10.16. YouVersion. 2025. App.
5. Holy Bible. New International Reader's Version. NIrV Bible. Version 10.16. YouVersion. 2025. App.
6. Holy Bible. King James Version. KJV. Version 10.16. YouVersion. 2025. App.
7. Holy Bible. New International Reader's Version. NIrV Bible. Version 10.16. YouVersion. 2025. App.

Bucket

1. Smith, Will. "How I Became The Fresh Prince of Bel-Air." YouTube, uploaded by willsmith, 5 May 2018, https://youtu.be/y_WoOYybCro?si=bEtKpic2873SkzP7. Accessed 12 Jun 2025.
2. ABC News. "Obama's New Policy List Rhymes with 'Bucket List.'" YouTube, uploaded by abcnews, 26 Apr 2015, https://youtu.be/ZRqSLz_6uEE?si=CJ5HmmliGTCL8d2j. Accessed 12 Jun 2025.
3. Holy Bible. New International Reader's Version. NIrV Bible. Version 10.16. YouVersion. 2025. App.

Unfun Forgiveness

1. Holy Bible. New International Reader's Version. NIrV Bible. Version 10.16. YouVersion. 2025. App.
2. Holy Bible. New International Reader's Version. NIrV Bible. Version 10.16. YouVersion. 2025. App.

Dis-Located

1. Holy Bible. New International Reader's Version. NIrV Bible. Version 10.16. YouVersion. 2025. App.

The Best Part

1. Maze, Frankie Beverly. "Joy and Pain. Joy and Pain, Capitol Records, 1980. CD
2. Holy Bible. New International Reader's Version. NIrV Bible. Version 10.16.

YouVersion. 2025. App.

³ Holy Bible. New International Version. NIV Bible. Version 10.16. YouVersion. 2025. App.

Egairram

¹ Steve Harvey: Don't Trip, He Ain't Through With Me Yet. Directed by Leslie Small, Uni Dust Corp, 2006.

² Holy Bible. New International Reader's Version. NIrV Bible. Version 10.16. YouVersion. 2025. App.

Oh Boy

¹ Kirk Franklin [kirkfranklin]. "Fear is nothing but contaminated faith. It's believing what the enemy says. FAITH is believing what GOD says. Who will u believe today? Go." X, 21 December 2012, 9:26 a.m., https://x.com/kirkfranklin/status/282129987312701440?s=46&t=fWIhBboarwLNCWxmbmXCkQ. Accessed 12 Jun. 2025.

Ready Ain't Waiting for You

¹ Holy Bible. New International Reader's Version. NIrV Bible. Version 10.16. YouVersion. 2025. App.

² Holy Bible. New International Reader's Version. NIrV Bible. Version 10.16. YouVersion. 2025. App.

³ Meyer, Joyce. "You Can't Pay for Something Twice." YouTube, uploaded by joycemeyer, 27 Jul. 2023, https://www.youtube.com/shorts/I44shkJ2a70. Accessed 8 Jun 2025.

⁴ Holy Bible. New International Reader's Version. NIrV Bible. Version 10.16. YouVersion. 2025. App.

⁵ Holy Bible. New International Reader's Version. NIrV Bible. Version 10.16. YouVersion. 2025. App.

⁶ Holy Bible. New International Reader's Version. NIrV Bible. Version 10.16. YouVersion. 2025. App.

Fear vs Ready

¹ Holy Bible. New International Reader's Version. NIrV Bible. Version 10.16. YouVersion. 2025. App.

* * *

Just Another Tuesday

[1] Holy Bible. New International Reader's Version. NIrV Bible. Version 10.16. YouVersion. 2025. App.

[2] Sinek, Simon. "There's no such thing as a plan that goes according to plan. #simonsinek #infinitemindset #leadership #optimism. TikTok, 22 Dec. 2021. https://www.tiktok.com/@simonsinek/video/7044657075674156334?_r=1&_t=ZT-8v9P2OyJJyo. Accessed 8 Jun. 2025.

[3] Holy Bible. New International Reader's Version. NIrV Bible. Version 10.16. YouVersion. 2025. App.

Unwanted Grace

[1] Holy Bible. New International Reader's Version. NIrV Bible. Version 10.16. YouVersion. 2025. App.

[2] Holy Bible. New International Reader's Version. NIrV Bible. Version 10.16. YouVersion. 2025. App.